everyday
Vegetarian

everyday
Vegetarian

MURDOCH
BOOKS

contents

The Vegetarian Choice

People can be drawn to a vegetarian diet for a variety of reasons. Some have ethical or health concerns, for others it is a matter of religious belief. But for many the decision to stop eating meat could just as easily be an aesthetic or gastronomic one. The variety of fresh seasonal ingredients, abundance of possible dishes and scope that vegetarian cuisine offers for creative cooking and eating are often dismissed or not recognised by confirmed meat-eaters.

For many in the developed world, meat has always been the easy option. Certainly meat dishes have appeared through the ages as the centrepiece of most meals. This tradition has led to a diet often lacking in variety and, consequently, in a beneficial balance of nutrients, as well as to the health consequences of eating too many saturated fats. A diet that over-emphasises meat is a product of affluence, and not necessarily a good one.

Many people have recognised an imbalance in their way of eating and are modifying the amount of flesh foods included in their diets. The discovery of vegetarian food often begins in this way. As people gain confidence, experiment more and discover the pleasures of cooking vegetarian foods they often welcome increased vitality and say goodbye to weight problems. Other benefits might be clearer skin and a more regular and comfortable bowel. Many choose to abandon eating meat altogether.

The term 'vegetarian' is used quite loosely. Some people call themselves vegetarian or 'semi-vegetarian' while still eating a little fish or chicken and no red meat. Many just exclude all meat and fish from their diets. Vegans, on the other hand, exclude all other animal products such as milk, cheese and eggs as well. Most vegetarians, however, are lacto-ovo vegetarians who still eat eggs and dairy products.

This book features no flesh foods, or products from them such as fish sauce or shrimp paste. It is not specifically a vegan cookbook, in that dairy foods such as eggs, butter, cheese and cream are used liberally. However, there are plenty of recipes that are suitable for vegans, particularly in the grains, pulses and tofu chapter. Nor is this a book of vegetarian substitutes for a meat-centred diet, offering recipes for pale imitations of meatloaf or burgers, or fake meat flavourings. The recipes are for anyone who loves preparing, serving and eating good food. It is neither a diet nor a health-food book, but is designed to expand the menu of possibilities, to show that one can be a connoisseur of good food, a fine cook and a vegetarian.

THE VEGETARIAN HEALTHY FOOD PYRAMID

If you were raised a vegetarian (and children thrive on a vegetarian diet), you are probably already in the habit of making sure all your nutritional needs are met. But for those just making the transition, there are a few things to bear in mind. It is just as possible to have a poor diet eating exclusively vegetarian foods as it is eating excessive amounts of animal products. The vegetarian healthy food pyramid is a good starting point if you want to check whether your diet is adequate. Its principles are simple:

EAT MOST
GRAINS: wheat, rice, barley, corn, oats, rye, millet, buckwheat
FOODS MADE FROM GRAINS: pasta, bread, wholegrain breakfast cereals
FRUIT AND VEGETABLES

EAT MODERATELY
DAIRY: milk, yoghurt, cheese
PULSES: peas, beans of all kinds, lentils
NUTS
EGGS

EAT LEAST
SUGARS: sugar, honey
FATS: butter, cream, margarine, oils, coconut milk
STIMULANTS: alcohol, tea, coffee

Meal-planning becomes easier if you make a habit of glancing at the food pyramid as a guide. There should be in each day a majority of foods from the 'Eat Most' group: fruit, cereals and toast for breakfast, bread or bread rolls, salads or cooked vegetable dishes and fruit for lunch or dinner; and pasta or rice-based main course for your largest meal (whether that's at lunchtime or in the evening) with fresh bread or rolls, and more fruit for dessert or snacks.

Small amounts of dairy foods from the 'Eat Moderately' group should form part of the day's meals (unless, or course, you are a vegan): yoghurt with breakfast or lunch, a little cheese with lunch or dinner. Being a vegetarian certainly doesn't mean going hungry: your main meal should include plenty of carbohydrate and protein—dishes and hearty soups made from beans or lentils, as well as egg dishes. Nuts are great for snacking.

The 'Eat Least' category means exactly that—a little butter or margarine on your breakfast toast, a drizzle of virgin olive oil with the salad

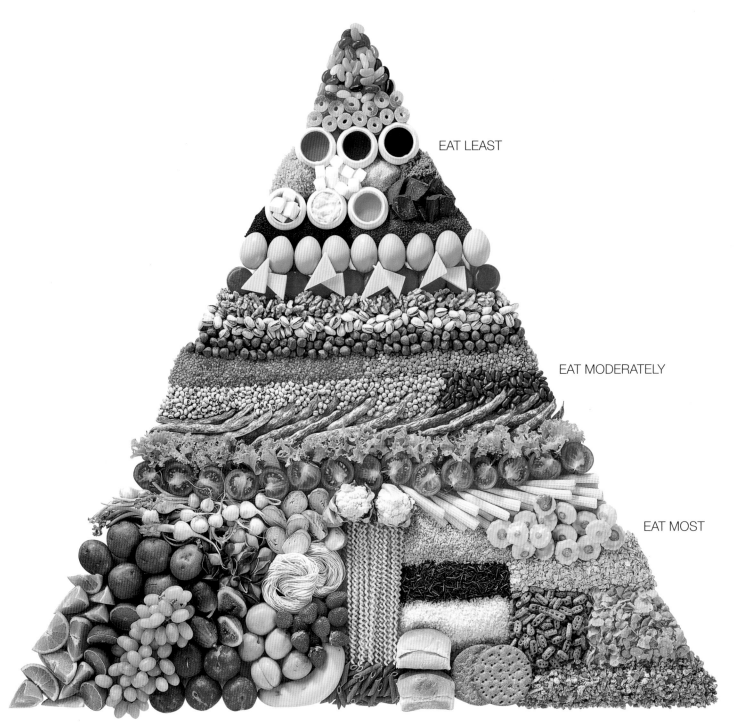

EAT LEAST

EAT MODERATELY

EAT MOST

The vegetarian pyramid

or to stir-fry the evening meal, a glass of wine with dinner. Like most things in life, sugary treats are fine, as long as they are enjoyed in moderation. You can balance the nutritional content of the day's meals so that the overall pattern easily satisfies the food pyramid guidelines. Compensate for an unavoidably fatty lunch, for example, with an evening meal made up of vegetables, grains and fruit.

snacks

MINI FRITTATAS

Preparation time: 30 minutes
Total cooking time: 45 minutes
Makes 12

1 kg (2 lb) orange sweet potato
1 tablespoon oil
30 g (1 oz) butter
4 leeks, white part only,
    finely sliced
2 cloves garlic, crushed
250 g (8 oz) feta cheese, crumbled
8 eggs
1/2 cup (125 ml/4 fl oz) cream

1 Preheat the oven to moderate 180°C (350°F/Gas 4). Grease or brush twelve 1 cup (250 ml/8 fl oz) muffin holes with oil or melted butter. Cut small rounds of baking paper and place into the base of each hole. Cut the sweet potato into small cubes and boil, steam or microwave until tender. Drain well and set aside.

2 Heat the oil and butter in a frying pan and cook the leek for 10 minutes, stirring occasionally, or until very soft and lightly golden. Add the garlic and cook for a further 1 minute. Cool, then stir in the feta and sweet potato. Divide among the muffin holes.

3 Whisk the eggs and cream together and season with salt and cracked black pepper. Pour the egg mixture into each hole until three-quarters filled, then press the vegetables down gently. Bake for 25–30 minutes, or until golden and set. Leave in the tins for 5 minutes, then ease out with a knife. Delicious either served hot or at room temperature.

NUTRITION PER FRITTATA
Protein 10 g; Fat 15 g; Carbohydrate 13 g; Dietary Fibre 2.5 g; Cholesterol 155 mg; 1000 kJ (240 cal)

Cut small rounds of baking paper and put one in the base of each muffin hole.

Spoon the vegetable mixture evenly into the muffin holes.

Whisk the eggs and cream together, season and pour into the muffin holes.

BLUE CHEESE AND PORT PATE

Preparation time: 10 minutes +
  refrigeration
Total cooking time: Nil
Serves 8

350 g (11 oz) cream cheese, at room
  temperature
60 g (2 oz) unsalted butter, softened
1/3 cup (80 ml/2³/₄ fl oz) port
300 g (10 oz) blue cheese, at room
  temperature, mashed
1 tablespoon snipped fresh chives
45 g (1¹/₂ oz) walnut halves

1 Using electric beaters, beat the
cream cheese and butter until smooth,
then stir in the port. Add the mashed
blue cheese and chives, and stir until
everything is just combined. Season
to taste with salt and freshly ground
black pepper.
2 Spoon the mixture into a serving
bowl and smooth the surface. Cover
the pâté with plastic wrap and
refrigerate until firm.
3 Arrange the walnuts over the top of
the pâté, pressing down lightly. Serve
at room temperature with fresh crusty
bread, crackers and celery sticks.

NUTRITION PER SERVE
Protein 12 g; Fat 37 g; Carbohydrate 2.5 g;
Dietary Fibre 0.5 g; Cholesterol 100 mg;
1650 kJ (395 Cal)

Stir the blue cheese and chives into the cream
cheese and butter mixture.

Arrange the walnut halves over the surface,
pressing down lightly.

TAMARI NUT MIX

Preparation time: 15 minutes
Total cooking time: 25 minutes
Serves 10–12

250 g (8 oz) mixed nuts (almonds,
  brazil nuts, peanuts, walnuts)
125 g (4 oz) pepitas (see NOTE)
125 g (4 oz) sunflower seeds
125 g (4 oz) cashew nuts
125 g (4 oz) macadamias
½ cup (125 ml/4 fl oz) tamari

1 Preheat the oven to very slow 140°C (275°F/Gas 1). Lightly grease two large baking trays.
2 Place the mixed nuts, pepitas, sunflower seeds, cashew nuts and macadamia nuts in a large bowl. Pour the tamari over the nuts and seeds and toss together, coating them evenly in the tamari. Leave for 10 minutes.
3 Spread the nut and seed mixture evenly over the baking trays and bake for 20–25 minutes, or until dry roasted. Cool completely and store in an airtight container for up to 2 weeks.

NUTRITION PER SERVE (12)
Protein 13 g; Fat 36 g; Carbohydrate 5.5 g; Dietary Fibre 5 g; Cholesterol 0 mg; 1620 kJ (385 Cal)

NOTE: Pepitas are peeled pumpkin seeds—they are available at most supermarkets and health-food stores.

STORAGE: Once stored, the nuts may become soft. If they do, spread them out flat on a baking tray and bake in a slow (150°C/300°F/Gas 2) oven for 5–10 minutes.

Stir the tamari through the nuts, pepitas and sunflower seeds.

Spread the nut mixture evenly over two lightly greased baking trays.

Dry-roast the tamari-coated nuts in the oven for 20–25 minutes.

ARTICHOKE AND PROVOLONE QUICHES

Preparation time: 40 minutes +
30 minutes refrigeration
Total cooking time: 35 minutes
Makes 6

2 cups (250 g/8 oz) plain flour
125 g (4 oz) butter, chilled and cubed
1 egg yolk
3 tablespoons iced water

FILLING
1 small eggplant, sliced
6 eggs, lightly beaten
3 teaspoons wholegrain mustard
150 g (5 oz) provolone cheese, grated
200 g (6^1/$_2$ oz) marinated artichokes, sliced
125 g (4 oz) semi-dried tomatoes

1 Process the flour and butter in a processor for about 15 seconds until crumbly. Add the egg yolk and water. Process in short bursts until the mixture comes together. Add a little more water if needed. Turn out onto a floured surface and gather into a ball. Wrap in plastic and refrigerate for at least 30 minutes.
2 Preheat the oven to 190°C (375°F/ Gas 5) and grease six 11 cm (4^1/$_2$ inch) oval pie tins.
3 To make the filling, brush the eggplant with olive oil and grill until golden. Mix together the eggs, mustard and cheese.
4 Roll out the pastry to line the tins. Trim the excess pastry and decorate the edges. Place one eggplant slice in each tin and top with artichokes and tomatoes. Pour the egg mixture over the top and bake for 25 minutes, or until golden.

NUTRITION PER QUICHE
Protein 20 g; Fat 30 g; Carbohydrate 35 g; Dietary Fibre 4 g; Cholesterol 290 mg; 2025 kJ (480 cal)

Gather the pastry into a ball and then wrap in plastic to refrigerate.

Brush each slice of eggplant with a little olive oil and then grill until golden.

Place one slice of eggplant in the bottom of each tin, then top with artichokes and tomatoes.

BOREKAS

Preparation time: 30 minutes
Total cooking time: 20 minutes
Makes 24

225 g (7 oz) feta cheese, crumbled
200 g (6½ oz) cream cheese, slightly softened
2 eggs, lightly beaten
¼ teaspoon ground nutmeg
20 sheets filo pastry
60 g (2 oz) butter, melted
3 tablespoons sesame seeds

1 Preheat the oven to moderate 180°C (350°F/Gas 4). Place the feta, cream cheese, egg and nutmeg in a bowl and mix until just combined—the mixture will be lumpy.

2 Work with five sheets of pastry at a time, keeping the rest covered with a damp tea towel. Lay each sheet on a work surface, brush with melted butter and lay them on top of each other. Use a ruler as guidance to cut the filo into six equal strips.

3 Place 1 tablespoon of the filling at one end of a strip, leaving a narrow border. Fold the pastry over to enclose the filling and form a triangle.

Continue folding the triangle over until you reach the end of the pastry, tucking any excess pastry under. Repeat with the remaining ingredients to make 24 triangles, and place on a lined baking tray.

4 Lightly brush with the remaining melted butter and sprinkle with sesame seeds. Bake for 15–20 minutes, or until puffed and golden.

NUTRITION PER BOREKA
Protein 4.5 g; Fat 8.5 g; Carbohydrate 6.5 g; Dietary Fibre 0.5 g; Cholesterol 35 mg; 505 kJ (120 cal)

Mix together the feta, cream cheese, egg and nutmeg until just combined.

Using a straight edge for guidance, cut the filo sheets into six even strips.

Fold the pastry over the filling, then continue folding until the end.

TOFU PASTRIES

Preparation time: 30 minutes +
  4 hours refrigeration
Total cooking time: 20 minutes
Serves 4

150 g (5 oz) firm tofu
2 spring onions, chopped
3 teaspoons chopped fresh coriander
  leaves
1/2 teaspoon grated orange rind
2 teaspoons soy sauce
1 tablespoon sweet chilli sauce
2 teaspoons grated fresh ginger
1 teaspoon cornflour
1/4 cup (60 g/2 oz) sugar
1/2 cup (125 ml/4 fl oz) rice vinegar

1 small Lebanese cucumber,
  finely diced
1 small red chilli, thinly sliced
1 spring onion, extra, thinly sliced on
  the diagonal
2 sheets ready-rolled puff pastry
1 egg, lightly beaten

1 Drain the tofu, then pat dry and cut into small cubes.
2 Put the spring onion, coriander, rind, soy and chilli sauces, ginger, cornflour and tofu in a bowl and gently mix. Cover, then refrigerate for 3–4 hours.
3 To make the dipping sauce, place the sugar and vinegar in a small saucepan and stir over low heat until the sugar dissolves. Remove from the heat and add the cucumber, chilli and extra spring onion. Cool completely.
4 Preheat the oven to hot 220°C (425°F/Gas 7). Cut each pastry sheet into four squares. Drain the filling and divide into eight. Place one portion in the centre of each square and brush the edges with egg. Fold into a triangle and seal the edges with a fork.
5 Put the triangles on two lined baking trays, brush with egg and bake for 15 minutes. Serve with the sauce.

NUTRITION PER SERVE
Protein 9 g; Fat 24 g; Carbohydrate 48 g;
Dietary Fibre 2 g; Cholesterol 66 mg;
1946 kJ (464 cal)

Gently mix the tofu and other ingredients together in a bowl.

Remove the saucepan from the heat and add the spring onion, cucumber and chilli.

Fold the pastry to enclose the filling, then seal the edges with a fork.

CORN MUFFINS

Preparation time: 20 minutes
Total cooking time: 25 minutes
Makes 12

2¹/₂ cups (310 g/10 oz) self-raising
   flour
¹/₂ cup (75 g/2¹/₂ oz) cornmeal
1 cup (250 ml/8 fl oz) milk
125 g (4 oz) butter, melted
2 eggs, lightly beaten
130 g (4¹/₂ oz) can corn kernels,
   drained
2 spring onions, finely chopped
¹/₂ cup (60 g/2 oz) grated Cheddar

1 Preheat the oven to hot 210°C
(415°F/Gas 6–7). Grease two trays
of six ¹/₂-cup (125 ml/4 fl oz) muffin
holes with butter. Sift the flour and
cornmeal into a large bowl and make a
well in the centre.
2 Whisk together the milk, butter,
eggs, corn, spring onion, Cheddar and
salt and pepper in a separate bowl and
pour into the well. Fold gently with a
metal spoon until all the ingredients
are just combined. Do not overmix—
the mixture should still be very lumpy.
3 Spoon the mixture into the tin and
bake for 20–25 minutes, or until lightly
golden. Leave for 5 minutes before
removing from the tin. Serve split in
half and spread with butter or cream
cheese. Delicious either hot or at
room temperature.

NUTRITION PER MUFFIN
Protein 6 g; Fat 12 g; Carbohydrate 27 g;
Dietary Fibre 1.5 g; Cholesterol 65 mg;
1009 kJ (240 cal)

VARIATION: Muffins are so versatile,
you can virtually add whatever you
have in the cupboard. Try adding
2 tablespoons chopped chives, ¹/₄ cup
(40 g/1¹/₄ oz) chopped, drained
sun-dried tomatoes or capsicum in oil,
2 finely chopped red chillies or
¹/₂ finely chopped red or green
capsicum into the mixture with the
milk and Cheddar.

STORAGE TIME: Store the muffins in
an airtight container for up to 2 days.

Trim the tops and tails from the spring onions and
then chop finely.

Sift the flour and cornmeal into a large bowl and
make a well in the centre.

Pour the milk mixture into the well in the dry
ingredients and fold gently until just combined.

Spoon the dough into the muffin holes and bake
until lightly golden.

SWEET POTATO AND LENTIL PASTRY POUCHES

Preparation time: 45 minutes
Total cooking time: 55 minutes
Makes 32

2 tablespoons olive oil
1 large leek, finely chopped
2 cloves garlic, crushed
125 g (4 oz) button mushrooms, roughly chopped
2 teaspoons ground cumin
2 teaspoons ground coriander
1/2 cup (95 g/3 oz) brown or green lentils
1/2 cup (125 g/4 oz) red lentils
2 cups (500 ml/16 fl oz) vegetable stock
300 g (10 oz) sweet potato, diced
4 tablespoons finely chopped fresh coriander leaves
8 sheets ready-rolled puff pastry
1 egg, lightly beaten
1/2 leek, extra, cut into thin strips
200 g (61/2 oz) plain yoghurt
2 tablespoons grated Lebanese cucumber
1/2 teaspoon soft brown sugar

1 Preheat the oven to moderately hot 200°C (400°F/Gas 6). Heat the oil in a saucepan over medium heat and cook the leek for 2–3 minutes, or until soft. Add the garlic, mushrooms, cumin and ground coriander and cook for 1 minute, or until fragrant.
2 Add the combined lentils and stock and bring to the boil. Reduce the heat and simmer for 20–25 minutes, or until the lentils are cooked through, stirring occasionally. Add the sweet potato in the last 5 minutes.
3 Transfer to a bowl and stir in the coriander. Season to taste. Cool.

4 Cut the pastry sheets into four even squares. Place 11/2 tablespoons of filling into the centre of each square and bring the edges together to form a pouch. Pinch together, then tie each pouch with string. Lightly brush with egg and place on lined baking trays. Bake for 20–25 minutes, or until the pastry is puffed and golden.
5 Soak the leek strips in boiling water for 30 seconds. Remove the string and re-tie with a piece of blanched leek. Put the yoghurt, cucumber and sugar in a bowl and mix together well. Serve with the pastry pouches.

NUTRITION PER PASTRY POUCH
Protein 5 g; Fat 11 g; Carbohydrate 20 g;
Dietary Fibre 2 g; Cholesterol 17 mg;
835 kJ (200 cal)

Stir the coriander leaves into the cooked lentils and sweet potato.

Put the filling in the centre of each square, form a pouch and tie with string.

Blanch the long strips of leek by soaking them for 30 seconds in boiling water.

17

VEGETABLE SAMOSAS

Preparation time: 35 minutes +
  20 minutes refrigeration
Total cooking time: 30 minutes
Makes 32

4 cups (500 g/1 lb) plain flour
2 tablespoons oil
oil, for deep-frying

VEGETABLE FILLING
600 g (1¼ lb) waxy potatoes
185 g (6 oz) cauliflower florets,
  chopped
2 tablespoons vegetable oil
1 onion, chopped
2 cloves garlic, finely chopped
2 tablespoons grated fresh ginger
2 tablespoons mild curry powder
⅔ cup (100 g/3½ oz) frozen peas
2 tablespoons lemon juice

1 In a food processor, process the
flour and 1 teaspoon of salt for
5 seconds. Add the combined oil
and 1 cup (250 ml/8 fl oz) of warm
water. Process in short bursts until the
mixture just comes together. Turn out
onto a floured surface and gather into
a ball. Cover with plastic wrap and
refrigerate for 20 minutes.
2 To make the filling, chop the
potatoes into quarters, cook until
tender, then cool and finely dice. Boil
or steam the cauliflower until tender,
cool and finely dice. Heat the oil in a
large frying pan and cook the onion
over medium heat for 5 minutes, or
until soft. Add the garlic, ginger and
curry powder and cook for 2 minutes.
Add the potato, cauliflower, peas and
lemon juice and mix well. Remove
from the heat and cool.
3 Divide the dough into 16 portions.

On a lightly floured surface, roll each
portion into a 15 cm (6 inch) round,
cut the rounds in half and put a
tablespoon of the mixture in the
middle of each semi-circle. Brush the
edge with water and fold the pastry
over the mixture, pressing to seal.
4 Heat a deep-fat fryer, or fill a deep
pan one-third full of oil and heat to
180°C (350°F) until a cube of bread
browns in 15 seconds. Deep-fry the

samosas in batches for 1 minute, or
until golden. Drain on paper towels
and serve hot with mango chutney,
sweet chilli sauce or natural yoghurt.

NUTRITION PER SAMOSA
Protein 2.5 g; Fat 6 g; Carbohydrate 15 g;
Dietary Fibre 1.5 g; Cholesterol 0 mg; 520 kJ
(125 Cal)

Process the flour, salt, oil and water until the
mixture just comes together.

Add the potato, cauliflower, peas and lemon juice
to the onion mixture.

Brush the edge of the dough with water, then fold
the filling over the top and seal.

SPICY CORN PUFFS

Preparation time: 25 minutes +
  10 minutes standing
Total cooking time: 15 minutes
Makes about 36

2 corn cobs
3 tablespoons chopped fresh
  coriander leaves
6 spring onions, finely chopped
1 small fresh red chilli, seeded and
  finely chopped
1 large egg
2 teaspoons ground cumin
1/2 teaspoon ground coriander
1 cup (125 g/4 oz) plain flour
oil, for deep-frying
sweet chilli sauce, to serve

1 Cut down the side of the corn cobs with a very sharp knife to release the kernels. Roughly chop the kernels, then place them in a large bowl. Holding the cobs over the bowl, scrape down the sides of the cobs with a knife to release all of the corn juice from the cob.

2 Add the fresh coriander, spring onion, chilli, egg, cumin, ground coriander, 1 teaspoon salt and freshly cracked black pepper to taste to the bowl, and stir well. Add the flour and mix well. The texture of the batter will vary depending on how much juice is released from the corn. If the mixture is too dry, add 1 tablespoon water, but no more than that as the batter should be quite thick and dry. Stand for 10 minutes.

3 Fill a large heavy-based saucepan or deep-fryer one-third full of oil and heat to 180°C (350°F), or until a cube of bread dropped in the oil browns in 15 seconds. Drop slightly heaped teaspoons of the corn batter into the oil and cook for about 1 1/2 minutes, or until puffed and golden. Drain on crumpled paper towels and serve immediately with a bowl of the sweet chilli sauce to dip the puffs into.

NUTRITION PER CORN PUFF
Protein 1 g; Fat 3.5 g; Carbohydrate 4.5 g; Dietary Fibre 0.5 g; Cholesterol 5.5 mg; 225 kJ (55 Cal)

NOTE: The batter should be prepared just before serving, or the corn puffs may fall apart when cooked.

Cut down the sides of the corn cobs to get all the corn kernels.

Mix the flour into the rest of the batter; the batter will be quite dry.

Fry the corn puffs until they puff up and are beautifully golden.

TZATZIKI

Preparation time: 10 minutes +
 15 minutes standing
Total cooking time: Nil
Serves 12

2 Lebanese cucumbers
400 g (13 oz) Greek-style plain
 yoghurt
4 cloves garlic, crushed
3 tablespoons finely chopped fresh
 mint, plus extra to garnish
1 tablespoon lemon juice

1 Cut the cucumbers in half lengthways, scoop out the seeds and discard. Leave the skin on and coarsely grate the cucumber into a small colander. Sprinkle with salt and leave over a large bowl for 15 minutes to drain off any bitter juices.
2 Meanwhile, stir together the yoghurt, crushed garlic, mint and lemon juice.
3 Rinse the cucumber under cold water then, taking small handfuls, squeeze out any excess moisture. Combine the grated cucumber with the yoghurt mixture and season well.

Serve immediately with pitta or pide bread or as a sauce with chicken.

NUTRITION PER SERVE
Protein 1.6 g; Fat 1.2 g; Carbohydrate 2.3 g;
Dietary Fibre 0.5 g; Cholesterol 5.3 mg;
119 kJ (28 cal)

STORAGE: Will keep in an airtight container in the fridge for 2–3 days.

Cut the cucumbers in half and scoop out the seeds with a teaspoon.

Mix the yoghurt, crushed garlic, mint and lemon juice together.

Squeeze the grated cucumber to remove any excess moisture.

TURKISH BREAD WITH HERBED ZUCCHINI

Preparation time: 15 minutes
Total cooking time: 35 minutes
Makes 48

1/2 large loaf Turkish bread
1 tablespoon sesame seeds
1/2 cup (125 ml/4 fl oz) vegetable oil

HERBED ZUCCHINI
1 tablespoon olive oil
2 cloves garlic, finely chopped
4 x 100 g (3½ oz) small zucchini, roughly chopped
1 large carrot, thinly sliced
2 tablespoons chopped fresh flat-leaf parsley
2 tablespoons chopped fresh mint
2 teaspoons lemon juice
1/2 teaspoon ground cumin

1 Split the Turkish bread horizontally through the middle and open it out. Cut the bread into 3 cm (1¼ inch) squares; you should end up with 48 squares.

2 Toast the sesame seeds in a large dry non-stick frying pan over low heat for 2–3 minutes, or until golden. Remove from the pan. Heat the vegetable oil in the same pan and cook the bread in batches for 1–2 minutes each side, or until crisp and golden. Drain on crumpled paper towels.

3 Heat the olive oil in a saucepan over medium heat and cook the garlic for 1 minute. Add the zucchini and carrot and cook over medium heat for 2 minutes. Season with salt and ground black pepper. Add 1 tablespoon water, cover and simmer over low heat for 15 minutes, or until the vegetables

are soft. Spoon into a bowl and mash roughly with a potato masher. Add the parsley, mint, lemon juice and cumin. Season to taste.

4 Spoon 2 teaspoons of the zucchini mixture over each square of bread and scatter with sesame seeds. Serve warm or at room temperature.

NUTRITION PER PIECE
Protein 0.5 g; Fat 2.5 g; Carbohydrate 2 g; Dietary Fibre 0.5 g; Cholesterol 0 mg; 140 kJ (35 Cal)

THINK AHEAD: The herbed zucchini can be prepared up to 2 days in advance. Reheat just before serving.

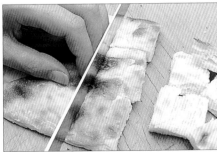

Split the bread in half horizontally, then cut it into 3 cm (1¼ inch) squares.

Use a potato masher to mash the zucchini and carrot mixture.

LENTIL RISSOLES

Preparation time: 20 minutes +
  40 minutes cooling
Total cooking time: 45 minutes
Serves 4

1 tablespoon oil
1 onion, finely chopped
2 large cloves garlic, crushed
2 teaspoons ground cumin
1 teaspoon ground coriander
1 small carrot, finely diced
1 cup (250 g/8 oz) red lentils
1¹/₂ cups (120 g/4 oz) fresh
  wholemeal breadcrumbs
²/₃ cup (60 g/2 oz) walnuts, finely
  chopped
¹/₂ cup (90 g/3 oz) frozen peas
3 tablespoons chopped fresh flat-leaf
  parsley
dry breadcrumbs, for coating
oil, for shallow-frying

1 Heat the oil in a large saucepan.
Cook the onion, garlic, cumin and
ground coriander over medium heat
for 2 minutes, or until the onion has
softened. Stir in the carrot, lentils and
2 cups (500 ml/16 fl oz) water. Slowly
bring to the boil, then reduce the heat
to low and simmer, covered, for
25–30 minutes, or until the lentils are
cooked and pulpy, stirring frequently
to stop them sticking and burning.
Remove the lid during the last
10 minutes to evaporate any
remaining liquid.
2 Transfer the mixture to a large
bowl, cover with plastic wrap and
cool for 10 minutes. Stir in the fresh
breadcrumbs, walnuts, peas and
parsley. Form into eight 8 cm (3 inch)

round rissoles. Cover and refrigerate
for 30 minutes, or until they are firm.
3 Evenly coat the rissoles in dry
breadcrumbs, shaking off any excess.
Heat 1 cm (¹/₂ inch) oil in a deep
frying pan, add the rissoles and cook
in two batches for 3 minutes each side,
or until golden brown. Drain on
crumpled paper towels, season
with salt and serve with a salad.

NUTRITION PER SERVE
Protein 24 g; Fat 20 g; Carbohydrate 50 g;
Dietary Fibre 14 g; Cholesterol 0 mg;
2014 kJ (480 Cal)

Cover the pan and simmer the lentils until they are
cooked and pulpy.

With clean hands, form the mixture into eight
round rissoles.

EGGPLANT AND CORIANDER TOSTADAS

Preparation time: 20 minutes
Total cooking time: 30 minutes
Serves 4

1 small eggplant, cut into cubes
1/2 red capsicum, cut into cubes
1/2 red onion, cut into thin wedges
2 tablespoons olive oil
1 large clove garlic, crushed
1 small loaf wood-fired bread, cut
    into 12 slices
1 small ripe tomato, halved
2 tablespoons chopped fresh mint

2 tablespoons chopped fresh
    coriander roots, stems and leaves
60 g (2 oz) slivered almonds, toasted

1 Preheat the oven to very hot 240°C (475°F/Gas 9). Put the eggplant, capsicum, onion and oil in a large bowl and mix to coat with the oil. Spread out in a single layer in a large roasting tin. Bake for 15 minutes, then turn and bake for a further 10 minutes, or until tender. Transfer to a bowl, add the garlic and season to taste with salt and black pepper.
2 Place the bread on a baking tray and bake for 4 minutes, or until crisp. Rub the cut side of the tomato onto one side of each bread slice, squeezing the tomato to get as much liquid as possible, then finely chop the tomato flesh and add to the vegetables with the mint and coriander.
3 Spoon the vegetables onto the tomato side of the bread and sprinkle with the almonds. Serve immediately.

NUTRITION PER SERVE
Protein 10 g; Fat 18 g; Carbohydrate 34 g;
Dietary Fibre 5 g; Cholesterol 0 mg;
1415 kJ (340 Cal)

NOTE: You can roast the vegetables and toast the almonds up to a day ahead. Store in an airtight container.

Spread the oil-coated vegetables in a single layer in a large roasting tin.

Tip the roasted vegetables into a bowl and mix with the garlic and seasoning.

Rub the cut side of the tomato onto one side of each slice of bread.

BEETROOT HUMMUS

Preparation time: 15 minutes
Total cooking time: 40 minutes
Serves 8

500 g (1 lb) beetroot, trimmed
4 tablespoons olive oil
1 large onion, chopped
1 tablespoon ground cumin
400 g (13 oz) can chickpeas, drained
1 tablespoon tahini
1/3 cup (90 g/3 oz) plain yoghurt
3 cloves garlic, crushed
1/4 cup (60 ml/2 fl oz) lemon juice
1/2 cup (125 ml/4 fl oz) vegetable
    stock

1 Scrub the beetroot well. Bring a large saucepan of water to the boil and cook the beetroot for 40 minutes, or until soft and cooked through. Drain and cool slightly before peeling.
2 Meanwhile, heat 1 tablespoon of the oil in a frying pan over medium heat and cook the onion for 2 minutes, or until soft. Add the cumin and cook for a further 1 minute, or until fragrant.
3 Chop the beetroot and place in a food processor or blender with the onion mixture, chickpeas, tahini, yoghurt, garlic, lemon juice and stock, and process until smooth. With the motor running, add the remaining oil in a thin steady stream. Process until the mixture is thoroughly combined.

Spoon the hummus into a serving bowl and serve with Turkish bread.

NUTRITION PER SERVE
Protein 5 g; Fat 11.5 g; Carbohydrate 12 g;
Dietary Fibre 4.5 g; Cholesterol 1.5 mg;
725 kJ (175 Cal)

NOTE: Beetroot hummus can be a great accompaniment to a main meal or is delicious as part of a meze platter with bruschetta or crusty bread. Its vivid colour sparks up any table.

VARIATION: You can use 500 g (1 lb) of any vegetable to make the hummus. Try carrot or pumpkin.

Cook the beetroot until soft, then drain and cool slightly before peeling off the skins.

Cook the onion until soft, then add the cumin and cook until fragrant.

Put all the hummus ingredients in a food processor and blend until smooth.

COUSCOUS PATTIES

Preparation time: 35 minutes +
    15 minutes refrigeration +
    10 minutes standing
Total cooking time: 30 minutes
Makes 4

1 cup (185 g/6 oz) couscous
4 tablespoons oil
1 eggplant, finely diced
1 onion, finely chopped
1 clove garlic, crushed
2 teaspoons ground cumin
2 teaspoons ground coriander
1 red capsicum, finely diced
2 tablespoons chopped fresh
    coriander
2 teaspoons grated lemon rind

2 teaspoons lemon juice
100 g (3¹/2 oz) natural yoghurt
1 egg, lightly beaten
oil, for shallow-frying

1 Place the couscous in a bowl. Add 1 cup (250 ml/8 fl oz) of boiling water and leave for 10 minutes, or until all the water has been absorbed. Fluff up the grains with a fork.
2 Heat 2 tablespoons of the oil in a large frying pan and fry the eggplant until soft and golden, then place in a bowl. Heat 1 tablespoon of the oil in the pan. Add the onion, garlic, cumin and ground coriander. Cook over medium heat for 3–4 minutes, or until soft, then add to the bowl. Heat the remaining oil and cook the capsicum for 5 minutes, or until soft.

Place in the bowl and stir well.
3 Add the vegetable mixture to the couscous with the fresh coriander, lemon rind, lemon juice, yoghurt and egg. Season to taste and mix well.
4 Using damp hands, divide the mixture into four portions and form into large patties—they should be about 2 cm (³/4 inch) thick. Cover and refrigerate for 15 minutes. Shallow-fry the patties over medium heat for 5 minutes on each side, or until golden. Drain the patties well and serve with yoghurt.

NUTRITION PER PATTY
Protein 9 g; Fat 25 g; Carbohydrate 35 g; Dietary Fibre 4 g; Cholesterol 5 mg; 1760 kJ (420 Cal)

When the couscous has absorbed the water, fluff up the grains with a fork.

Season the patty mixture with salt and cracked pepper and mix well.

With damp hands, form the mixture into four large patties.

SALT AND PEPPER TOFU PUFFS

Preparation time: 15 minutes
Total cooking time: 10 minutes
Serves 4–6

2 x 190 g (6½ oz) packets fried
   tofu puffs
2 cups (250 g/8 oz) cornflour
2 tablespoons salt
1 tablespoon ground white pepper
2 teaspoons caster sugar
4 egg whites, lightly beaten
oil, for deep-frying (see NOTE)
½ cup (125 ml/4 fl oz) sweet chilli
   sauce
2 tablespoons lemon juice
lemon wedges, to serve

1 Cut the tofu puffs in half with a sharp knife, and pat dry with paper towels.

2 Mix the cornflour, salt, pepper and caster sugar in a large bowl.
3 Dip the tofu into the egg white in batches, then toss in the cornflour mixture, shaking off any excess.
4 Fill a deep heavy-based saucepan or wok one-third full of oil and heat to 180°C (350°F), or until a cube of bread dropped into the oil browns in 15 seconds. Cook the tofu in batches for 1–2 minutes, or until crisp. Drain well on crumpled paper towels.

Dip the tofu puffs in the egg white, then in the cornflour, shaking off any excess.

5 Combine the chilli sauce and lemon juice in a bowl. Serve immediately with the tofu puffs and lemon wedges.

NUTRITION PER SERVE (6)
Protein 5.5 g; Fat 10 g; Carbohydrate 44 g; Dietary Fibre 1 g; Cholesterol 0.5 mg; 1190 kJ (285 Cal)

NOTE: It is best to use a good-quality peanut oil to deep-fry the tofu puffs—the flavour will be slightly nutty.

Deep-fry the tofu in batches until crisp, then remove with a slotted spoon.

CALIFORNIA ROLLS

Preparation time: 35 minutes +
  15 minutes standing
Total cooking time: 10 minutes
Makes 30 pieces

500 g (1 lb) short-grain white rice
1/4 cup (60 ml/2 fl oz) rice vinegar
1 tablespoon caster sugar
5 nori sheets
1 large Lebanese cucumber, cut
  lengthways into long batons
1 avocado, thinly sliced
1 tablespoon black sesame seeds,
  toasted
30 g (1 oz) pickled ginger slices
1/2 cup (125 g/4 oz) mayonnaise
3 teaspoons wasabi paste
2 teaspoons soy sauce

1 Wash the rice under cold running water, tossing, until the water runs clear. Put the rice and 3 cups (750 ml/24 fl oz) water in a saucepan. Bring to the boil over low heat and cook for 5 minutes, or until tunnels form in the rice. Remove from the heat, cover and leave for 15 minutes.
2 Place the vinegar, sugar and 1 teaspoon salt in a small saucepan and stir over low heat until the sugar and salt dissolve.
3 Transfer the rice to a non-metallic bowl and use a wooden spoon to separate the grains. Make a slight well in the centre, slowly stir in the vinegar dressing, then cool a little.
4 Lay a nori sheet, shiny-side-down, on a bamboo mat or flat surface and spread out one-fifth of the rice, leaving a narrow border at one end. Arrange one-fifth of the cucumber, avocado, sesame seeds and ginger lengthways over the rice, keeping away from the border. Spread with some of the combined mayonnaise, wasabi and soy sauce and roll to cover the filling. Continue rolling tightly to join the edge, then hold it in place for a few seconds. Trim the ends and cut into slices. Serve with wasabi mayonnaise.

NUTRITION PER PIECE
Protein 1.5 g; Fat 3.5 g; Carbohydrate 15 g; Dietary Fibre 1 g; Cholesterol 1 mg; 405 kJ (95 Cal)

Cook the rice until tunnels appear, then cover and leave for 15 minutes.

Slowly pour the vinegar dressing into the rice and stir it through.

Spread the wasabi mayonnaise mixture over the vegetables and start rolling.

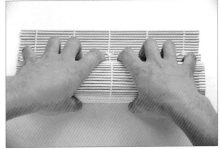
Roll the mat tightly to join the edge, then hold it in place for a few seconds.

BROWN RICE AND CASHEW PATTIES WITH CORIANDER SAMBAL

Preparation time: 30 minutes +
  overnight soaking + 30 minutes
  refrigeration
Total cooking time: 2 hours
Serves 8

250 g dried chickpeas
3 cups (650 g/1 lb 5 oz) instant brown
  rice (see NOTE)
1 tablespoon oil
1 onion, finely chopped
125 g (4 oz) roasted cashew paste
1 egg
60 g (2 oz) tahini
1 teaspoon ground cumin
1 teaspoon ground turmeric
1 tablespoon lemon juice
1 vegetable stock cube
5 tablespoons tamari
1 small carrot, grated
1/2 cup (40 g/11/2 oz) fresh wholemeal
  breadcrumbs
oil, for shallow-frying
2 tablespoons oil, extra
310 g (10 oz) bok choy, trimmed and
  washed

CORIANDER AND COCONUT
  SAMBAL
90 g (3 oz) fresh coriander leaves
1 clove garlic, chopped
1 small fresh green chilli, seeded and
  finely chopped
1 teaspoon garam masala
2 tablespoons lime juice
1/4 cup (15 g/1/2 oz) shredded coconut

1 Soak the chickpeas in cold water
overnight. Drain. Place in a large
saucepan and cover with water. Bring
to the boil and cook for 1–11/2 hours,
or until cooked. Drain, reserving

2 tablespoons of the liquid.
2 Meanwhile, bring a saucepan of
water to the boil and cook the rice
over medium heat for 10–12 minutes,
or until tender. Rinse well and drain.
Keep warm.
3 Heat the oil in a frying pan and
cook the onion for 2–3 minutes, or
until golden. Set aside.
4 Mix the chickpeas, cashew paste,
egg, tahini, cumin, turmeric, lemon
juice, stock cube, reserved chickpea
liquid and 2 tablespoons of the tamari
in a food processor until smooth.
Transfer to a large bowl and add the
rice, onion, carrot and breadcrumbs
and mix well. Divide the mixture into
16 even portions and form into patties
about 1.5 cm thick. Refrigerate for
30 minutes.
5 To make the sambal, finely chop all
the ingredients in a food processor.
Refrigerate until ready to use.
6 To cook the patties, heat the oil in a
large deep frying pan over medium
heat and cook in batches for
3–4 minutes each side, or until golden
and cooked through. Remove and
keep warm. Wipe with a paper towel.
In the same pan, heat the extra oil and
add the bok choy and cook, tossing,
for 1–2 minutes, or until wilted. Pour
on the remaining 3 tablespoons tamari
and toss through. Place the bok choy
on eight serving plates and top with
two patties. Spoon a dollop of chilled
sambal on top and serve immediately.

NUTRITION PER SERVE
Protein 17 g; Fat 17 g; Carbohydrate 80 g;
Dietary Fibre 11 g; Cholesterol 23 mg;
2294 kJ (548 cal)

NOTE: Instant (or quick-cook) rice has
been cooked, then dehydrated so it
takes less time to cook than the
ordinary type.

BABA GHANNOUJ

Preparation time: 20 minutes +
   30 minutes cooling
Total cooking time: 50 minutes
Serves 10

2 eggplants
3 cloves garlic, crushed
1/2 teaspoon ground cumin
1/3 cup (80 ml/2 3/4 fl oz) lemon juice
2 tablespoons tahini
pinch cayenne pepper
1 1/2 tablespoons olive oil
1 tablespoon finely chopped
   fresh flat-leaf parsley
black olives, to garnish

1 Preheat the oven to 200°C (400°F/
Gas 6). Pierce the eggplants several
times with a fork, then cook over an
open flame for about 5 minutes, or
until the skin is black and blistering,
then place in a roasting tin and bake
for 40–45 minutes, or until the
eggplants are very soft and wrinkled.
Place in a colander over a bowl to
drain off any bitter juices and leave to
stand for 30 minutes, or until cool.
2 Carefully peel the skin from the
eggplant, chop the flesh and place
in a food processor with the garlic,
cumin, lemon, tahini, cayenne and
olive oil. Process until smooth and
creamy. Alternatively, use a potato
masher or fork. Season with salt and
stir in the parsley. Spread onto a flat
bowl or plate and garnish with the
olives. Serve with flatbread or pide.

NUTRITION PER SERVE
Protein 1.8 g; Fat 5 g; Carbohydrate 3 g;
Dietary Fibre 3 g; Cholesterol 0 mg;
269 kJ (64 cal)

NOTE: If you prefer, you can simply
roast the eggplant in a roasting tin in a
200°C (400°F/Gas 6) oven for 1 hour,
or until very soft and wrinkled.
Eggplants are also known as
aubergines. The name baba ghannouj
can be roughly translated as 'poor
man's caviar'.

Carefully peel the black and blistered skin away
from the baked eggplant.

Process the eggplant, garlic, cumin, lemon,
tahini, cayenne and olive oil.

SPINACH AND FETA TRIANGLES

Preparation time: 30 minutes
Total cooking time: 40 minutes
Makes 8

1 kg (2 lb) English spinach
1/4 cup (60 ml/2 fl oz) olive oil
1 onion, chopped
10 spring onions, sliced
1/3 cup (20 g/3/4 oz) chopped fresh
    parsley
1 tablespoon chopped fresh dill
large pinch of ground nutmeg
1/3 cup (35 g/1 1/4 oz) freshly grated
    Parmesan
150 g (5 oz) crumbled feta cheese
90 g (3 oz) ricotta cheese
4 eggs, lightly beaten
40 g (1 1/4 oz) butter, melted
1 tablespoon olive oil, extra
12 sheets filo pastry

1 Trim any coarse stems from the spinach. Wash the leaves thoroughly, roughly chop and place in a large pan with just a little water clinging to the leaves. Cover and cook gently over low heat for 5 minutes, or until the leaves have wilted. Drain well and allow to cool slightly before squeezing tightly to remove the excess water.
2 Heat the oil in a heavy-based frying pan. Add the onion and cook over low heat for 10 minutes, or until tender and golden. Add the spring onion and cook for a further 3 minutes. Remove from the heat. Stir in the drained spinach, parsley, dill, ground nutmeg, Parmesan, feta, ricotta and egg. Season well.
3 Preheat the oven to moderate 180°C (350°F/Gas 4). Grease two baking trays. Combine the melted butter with the extra oil. Work with three sheets of pastry at a time, keeping the rest covered with a damp tea towel. Brush each sheet with butter mixture and lay them on top of each other. Cut each stack in half lengthways.
4 Spoon 4 tablespoons of the filling on an angle at the end of each strip. Fold the pastry over to enclose the filling and form a triangle. Continue folding the triangle over until your reach the end of the pastry. Put the triangles on the baking trays and brush with the remaining butter mixture. Bake for 20–25 minutes, or until the pastry is golden brown.

NUTRITION PER TRIANGLE
Protein 15 g; Fat 23 g; Carbohydrate 14 g;
Dietary Fibre 4 g; Cholesterol 135 mg;
1335 kJ (320 Cal)

NOTE: Feta is a salty Greek cheese that should be stored immersed in lightly salted water in the fridge. Rinse and pat dry before using.

VARIATION: If spinach isn't in season you can use silverbeet instead. Use the same quantity and trim the coarse white stems from the leaves.

Brush each sheet of filo pastry with the mixture of butter and oil.

Spoon the filling onto the end of the pastry at an angle. Fold the pastry over it to make a triangle.

Continue folding the triangle parcel until you reach the end of the pastry sheet.

CHARGRILLED POTATOES WITH PISTACHIO SALSA

Preparation time: 25 minutes
Total cooking time: 20 minutes
Serves 4

PISTACHIO SALSA
150 g (5 oz) pistachio nuts, toasted
2 ripe tomatoes, chopped
2 cloves garlic, finely chopped
1 small red chilli, finely chopped
2 tablespoons chopped fresh parsley
1 tablespoon chopped fresh mint
1 teaspoon finely grated lemon rind

750 g (1½ lb) potatoes
3 tablespoons plain flour
2 tablespoons olive oil
sour cream, to serve

1 To make the pistachio salsa, roughly chop the nuts and combine with the tomato, garlic, chilli, herbs and lemon rind. Season with salt and pepper.
2 Peel the potatoes and cut into large wedges. Place in a pan and cover with water, bring to the boil and cook for 5 minutes. Transfer to a colander and rinse under running water to stop the cooking. Pat the wedges dry with paper towels.

3 Sprinkle the flour over the potatoes in a bowl and toss to lightly coat. Cook the potato wedges in a single layer on a hot, lightly oiled barbecue flatplate or grill for 5–10 minutes, or until golden brown and tender. Drizzle with the olive oil and turn the potatoes regularly during cooking. Serve with the salsa and a bowl of sour cream.

NUTRITION PER SERVE
Protein 10 g; Fat 30 g; Carbohydrate 30 g;
Dietary Fibre 5 g; Cholesterol 0 mg;
1755 kJ (415 cal)

To make the salsa, simply mix together all the ingredients and season well.

Cut the potatoes into wedges and then boil for 5 minutes.

Cook the pototo wedges on the barbecue until they are golden brown.

CORN AND POLENTA PANCAKES WITH TOMATO SALSA

Preparation time: 15 minutes
Total cooking time: 10 minutes
Serves 4

TOMATO SALSA
2 ripe tomatoes
1 cup (150 g/5 oz) frozen broad beans
2 tablespoons chopped fresh basil
1 small Lebanese cucumber, diced
2 small cloves garlic, crushed
1 1/2 tablespoons balsamic vinegar
1 tablespoon extra virgin olive oil

CORN AND POLENTA PANCAKES
3/4 cup (90 g/3 oz) self-raising flour
3/4 cup (110 g/3 1/2 oz) fine polenta
1 cup (250 ml/8 fl oz) milk
310 g (10 oz) can corn kernels
olive oil, for frying

1 To make the salsa, score a cross in the base of each tomato, then place in a bowl of boiling water for 30 seconds. Plunge into cold water and peel the skin away from the cross. Dice. Pour boiling water over the broad beans and leave for 2–3 minutes. Drain and rinse under cold water. Remove the skins. Put the beans in a bowl and stir in the tomato, basil, cucumber, garlic, vinegar and extra virgin olive oil.

2 To make the pancakes, sift the flour into a bowl and stir in the polenta. Add the milk and corn and stir until just combined, adding more milk if the batter is too dry. Season.

3 Heat the oil in a large frying pan and spoon half the batter into the pan, making four 9 cm (3 1/2 inch) pancakes. Cook for 2 minutes each side, or until golden and cooked through. Repeat with the remaining batter, adding more oil if necessary. Drain well and serve with the salsa.

NUTRITION PER SERVE
Protein 11 g; Fat 18.5 g; Carbohydrate 56 g;
Dietary Fibre 8.5 g; Cholesterol 8.5 mg;
1809 kJ (432 cal)

After blanching, it will be easy to peel the skin off the broad beans.

Stir the milk and corn kernels into the flour and polenta mixture.

Cook the pancakes for 2 minutes each side, or until golden and cooked through.

ZUCCHINI AND HALOUMI FRITTERS

Preparation time: 15 minutes
Total cooking time: 25 minutes
Makes 45

300 g (10 oz) zucchini
4 spring onions, thinly sliced
200 g (6½ oz) haloumi, coarsely grated
¼ cup (30 g/1 oz) plain flour
2 eggs
1 tablespoon chopped fresh dill, plus sprigs, to garnish
¼ cup (60 ml/2 oz) oil
1 lemon, cut into very thin slices, seeds removed
⅓ cup (90 g/3 oz) thick Greek-style yoghurt

1 Coarsely grate the zucchini and squeeze out as much liquid as possible in your hands or in a clean tea towel.

Combine the zucchini with the spring onion, haloumi, flour, eggs and dill. Season well with salt and cracked black pepper.
2 Heat the oil in a large heavy-based frying pan. Form fritters (using heaped teaspoons of the mixture) and cook in batches for 2 minutes each side, or until golden and firm. Drain on crumpled paper towels.
3 Cut each slice of lemon into quarters or eighths, depending on the size, to make small triangles.
4 Top each fritter with ½ teaspoon yoghurt, a piece of lemon and a small sprig of dill.

NUTRITION PER FRITTER
Protein 1.5 g; Fat 4 g; Carbohydrate 1 g; Dietary Fibre 0 g; Cholesterol 12 mg; 170 kJ (40 Cal)

NOTE: The fritters are best prepared and cooked just before serving. If you allow them to sit, the haloumi tends to go a little tough.

Squeeze as much liquid as possible from the grated zucchini.

Cook the fritters until they are nicely golden on both sides.

DOLMADES

Preparation time: 40 minutes
 + 15 minutes soaking
Total cooking time: 45 minutes
Makes 24

200 g (6½ oz) packet vine leaves
 in brine
1 cup (250 g/8 oz) medium-grain rice
1 small onion, finely chopped
1 tablespoon olive oil
50 g (1¾ oz) pine nuts, toasted
2 tablespoons currants
2 tablespoons chopped fresh dill
1 tablespoon finely chopped fresh
 mint
1 tablespoon finely chopped fresh
 flat-leaf parsley
⅓ cup (80 ml/2¾ fl oz) olive oil, extra
2 tablespoons lemon juice
2 cups (500 ml/16 fl oz) vegetable
 stock

1 Place the vine leaves in a bowl, cover with hot water and soak for 15 minutes. Remove and pat dry. Cut off any stems. Reserve some leaves to line the saucepan and discard any with holes. Meanwhile, soak the rice in boiling water for 10 minutes to soften, then drain.
2 Place the rice, onion, oil, pine nuts, currants, herbs and some salt and pepper in a large bowl, and mix well.
3 Lay a leaf vein-side-down on a flat surface. Place 1 tablespoon of filling in the middle of the leaf, fold the stalk end over the filling, then the left and right sides into the middle, then roll firmly towards the tip. The dolmade should resemble a cigar. Repeat with the remaining filling and leaves.
4 Using the reserved vine leaves, line the bottom of a large heavy-based saucepan. Drizzle with 1 tablespoon of the extra oil. Place the dolmades in the pan, packing them tightly in one layer. Pour the lemon juice and remaining olive oil over them.
5 Pour the chicken stock over the dolmades and cover with an inverted plate to stop them moving around while cooking. Bring to the boil, then reduce the heat and simmer, covered, for 45 minutes. Remove with a slotted spoon. May be served warm or cold.

NUTRITION PER DOLMADE
Protein 1.5 g; Fat 4 g; Carbohydrate 9.5 g;
Dietary Fibre 0.5 g; Cholesterol 0 mg;
335 kJ (80 Cal)

NOTE: Any unused leaves can be stored in brine in an airtight container in the refrigerator for up to 1 week.

Fold the sides of the vine leaf into the middle and roll up towards the tip.

Pack the dolmades tightly into the pan and pour on the oil and lemon juice.

Remove the cooked dolmades from the pan with a slotted spoon.

BEAN NACHOS

Preparation time: 20 minutes
Total cooking time: 10 minutes
Serves 4

4 large ripe tomatoes
2 ripe avocados, mashed
1 tablespoon lime juice
1 tablespoon sweet chilli sauce
1 tablespoon oil
2 small red onions, diced
1 small red chilli, chopped
2 teaspoons ground oregano
2 teaspoons ground cumin
1/4 teaspoon chilli powder
1 tablespoon tomato paste

1 cup (250 ml/8 fl oz) white wine
2 x 440 g (14 oz) cans red kidney
   beans, rinsed and drained
3 tablespoons chopped fresh
   coriander leaves
200 g (6 1/2 oz) packet corn chips
2/3 cup (90 g/3 oz) grated Cheddar
sour cream, to serve

1 Score a cross in the base of each
tomato. Put them in a bowl of boiling
water for 30 seconds, then plunge
into cold water and peel the skin away
from the cross. Cut in half and scoop
out the seeds with a teaspoon. Chop
the tomato flesh.
2 Mix together the avocado, lime juice
and sweet chilli sauce.

3 Heat the oil in a large frying pan.
Cook the onion, chilli, oregano, cumin
and chilli powder over medium heat
for 2 minutes. Add the tomato, tomato
paste and wine and cook for 5 minutes,
or until the liquid reduces. Add the
beans and coriander.
4 Divide the corn chips into four
portions on heatproof plates. Top
with the bean mixture and sprinkle
with cheese. Flash under a hot grill
until the cheese melts. Serve with the
avocado mixture and sour cream.

NUTRITION PER SERVE
Protein 26 g; Fat 35 g; Carbohydrate 53 g;
Dietary Fibre 20 g; Cholesterol 20 mg;
2845 kJ (680 Cal)

Scoop out the seeds of the tomatoes and roughly
chop the flesh.

Cook the onion, chilli, oregano and spices in a
large frying pan.

Cook the mixture until the liquid is reduced and
the tomato is soft.

ONION BHAJIS WITH SPICY TOMATO SAUCE

Preparation time: 30 minutes
Total cooking time: 35 minutes
Makes about 25

SPICY TOMATO SAUCE
2–3 red chillies, chopped
1 red capsicum, diced
425 g (14 oz) can chopped tomatoes
2 cloves garlic, finely chopped
2 tablespoons soft brown sugar
1¹/₂ tablespoons cider vinegar

1 cup (125 g/4 oz) plain flour
2 teaspoons baking powder
¹/₂ teaspoon chilli powder
¹/₂ teaspoon ground turmeric
1 teaspoon ground cumin
2 eggs, beaten
1 cup (60 g/2 oz) chopped fresh
    coriander leaves
4 onions, very thinly sliced
oil, for deep-frying

1 To make the sauce, combine all the ingredients with 3 tablespoons water in a saucepan. Bring to the boil, then reduce the heat and simmer for 20 minutes, or until the mixture thickens. Remove from the heat.
2 To make the bhajis, sift the flour, baking powder, spices and 1 teaspoon salt into a bowl and make a well in the centre. Gradually add the combined egg and 3 tablespoons water, whisking to make a smooth batter. Stir in the coriander and onion.
3 Fill a deep heavy-based saucepan one-third full of oil and heat until a cube of bread dropped into the oil browns in 15 seconds. Drop dessertspoons of the mixture into the oil and cook in batches for 90 seconds each side, or until golden. Drain on paper towels. Serve with the spicy tomato sauce.

NUTRITION PER BHAJI
Protein 1.5 g; Fat 2 g; Carbohydrate 7 g;
Dietary Fibre 1 g; Cholesterol 14 mg;
218 kJ (52 cal)

Peel the four onions and use a sharp knife to slice them very thinly.

Simmer the spicy tomato sauce for 20 minutes, or until it thickens.

Whisk together a smooth batter, then add the sliced onion and coriander and stir to coat.

Drop spoonfuls of the onion batter into the oil and cook in batches until golden.

37

ROASTED ORANGE SWEET POTATO AND DITALINI PATTIES

Preparation time: 15 minutes
Total cooking time: 1 hour 10 minutes
Serves 4

2 orange sweet potatoes
(about 800 g/1 lb 10 oz in total)
1/2 cup (90 g/3 oz) ditalini
30 g (1 oz) toasted pine nuts
2 cloves garlic, crushed
4 tablespoons finely chopped
fresh basil
1/2 cup (50 g/1 3/4 oz) grated Parmesan
1/3 cup (35 g/1 1/4 oz) dry breadcrumbs
plain flour, for dusting
olive oil, for shallow-frying

1 Preheat the oven to very hot 250°C (500°F/Gas 10). Pierce the sweet potatoes several times with a fork, then place in a roasting tin and roast for about 1 hour, or until soft. Remove from the oven and cool. Meanwhile, cook the pasta in a large saucepan of boiling water until *al dente*. Drain and rinse under running water.
2 Peel the sweet potato and mash the flesh with a potato masher or fork, then add the pine nuts, garlic, basil, Parmesan, breadcrumbs and the pasta and combine. Season.
3 Shape the mixture into eight even patties (about 1.5 cm/5/8 inch thick) with floured hands, then lightly dust the patties with flour. Heat the oil in a large frying pan and cook the patties in batches over medium heat for

2 minutes each side, or until golden and heated through. Drain on crumpled paper towels, sprinkle with salt and serve immediately. Great with a fresh green salad.

NUTRITION PER SERVE
Protein 13.5 g; Fat 15 g; Carbohydrate 51 g; Dietary Fibre 5.5 g; Cholesterol 12 mg; 1650 kJ (395 Cal)

NOTE: To save time, drop spoonfuls of the mixture into the pan and flatten with an oiled spatula.

SERVING SUGGESTION: The patties are great with aïoli—mix 1 clove of crushed garlic into 1/3 cup (90 g/3 oz) whole-egg mayonnaise with a squeeze of lemon juice and season.

Test if the sweet potatoes are cooked with the point of a sharp knife.

When the sweet potatoes are cool enough to handle, peel them with your fingers.

Dusting your hands with flour before handling the mixture will prevent the patties from sticking.

CRISP POLENTA WITH MUSHROOMS

Preparation time: 30 minutes +
  30 minutes refrigeration
Total cooking time: 40 minutes
Serves 4

1 litre vegetable stock
1 cup (150 g/5 oz) polenta
2 tablespoons low-fat margarine
1 tablespoon grated fresh Parmesan
rocket, to serve
fresh Parmesan, shaved, to serve

MUSHROOM SAUCE
10 g (1/4 oz) dried porcini mushrooms
1 tablespoon olive oil
800 g (1 lb 10 oz) mixed mushrooms
  (field, Swiss brown), thickly sliced
4 cloves garlic, finely chopped
2 teaspoons chopped fresh thyme
3/4 cup (185 ml/6 fl oz) dry white wine
1/2 cup (125 ml/4 fl oz) vegetable stock
1/2 cup (30 g/1 oz) chopped fresh
  parsley

1 Bring the stock to the boil in a large saucepan. Add the polenta in a thin stream, stirring constantly. Simmer for 20 minutes over very low heat, stirring frequently, or until the mixture starts to leave the side of the pan. Add the margarine and Parmesan. Season. Grease a shallow 20 cm (8 inch) square cake tin. Pour in the polenta, smooth the surface and refrigerate for 30 minutes, or until set.
2 To make the mushroom sauce, soak the dried porcini mushrooms in 1/2 cup (125 ml/4 fl oz) boiling water for 10 minutes, or until softened. Drain, reserving 1/3 cup (80 ml/2 3/4 fl oz) of the liquid.
3 Heat the oil in a large frying pan. Add the mixed mushrooms and cook over high heat for 4–5 minutes, or until softened. Add the porcini, garlic and thyme, then season and cook for 2–3 minutes. Add the wine and cook until it has evaporated. Add the stock and soaking liquid, then reduce the heat and cook for a 3–4 minutes, or until the stock has reduced and thickened. Stir in the parsley.
4 Cut the polenta into 4 squares and grill until golden on both sides. Place one on each serving plate and top with the mushrooms. Garnish with rocket and Parmesan shavings.

NUTRITION PER SERVE
Protein 15 g; Fat 11 g; Carbohydrate 35 g;
Dietary Fibre 7 g; Cholesterol 1.5 mg;
1390 kJ (330 Cal)

Cook the porcini and mixed mushrooms over high heat until softened.

Grill squares of polenta until golden on both sides.

39

TEMPURA VEGETABLES WITH WASABI MAYONNAISE

Preparation time: 20 minutes
Total cooking time: 20 minutes
Serves 4–6

WASABI MAYONNAISE
2 tablespoons mayonnaise
3 teaspoons wasabi paste
1/2 teaspoon grated lime rind

2 egg yolks
1 cup (250 ml/8 fl oz) chilled soda
    water
1/4 cup (30 g/1 oz) cornflour
110 g (31/2 oz) plain flour
1/4 cup (40 g/11/4 oz) sesame seeds,
    toasted
oil, for deep-frying
1 small (250 g/8 oz) eggplant, sliced
    5 mm (1/4 inch) thick
1 large onion, sliced 5 mm (1/4 inch)
    thick, with rings intact
300 g (10 oz) orange sweet potato,
    sliced 5 mm (1/4 inch) thick

1 To make the wasabi mayonnaise, mix together all the ingredients. Cover with plastic wrap and refrigerate until ready to use.

2 Place the egg yolks and soda water in a jug and mix lightly with a whisk. Sift the cornflour and flour into a bowl. Add the sesame seeds and a good sprinkling of salt and mix well. Pour the soda water and egg yolk mixture into the flour and stir lightly with chopsticks or a fork until just combined but still lumpy.

3 Fill a deep heavy-based saucepan or wok one-third full of oil and heat until a cube of bread dropped into the oil browns in 15 seconds. Using tongs, pick up two pieces of vegetable together—eggplant and onion or sweet potato and onion or eggplant and sweet potato—and dip into the batter. Deep-fry for 3–4 minutes, or until golden brown and cooked through. Drain on crumpled paper towels and season well with salt. Keep warm, but do not cover or the batter will go soggy. Serve as soon as possible with the wasabi mayonnaise.

NUTRITION PER SERVE (6)
Protein 6 g; Fat 14 g; Carbohydrate 30 g;
Dietary Fibre 3.5 g; Cholesterol 62 mg;
1112 kJ (266 cal)

Gently stir the combined soda water and egg yolk into the flour mixture.

Pick up two different pieces of vegetable with tongs and dip into the batter.

Deep-fry the battered vegetables until they are golden brown and cooked through.

VEGETABLE CHIPS

Preparation time: 20 minutes
Total cooking time: 15 minutes
Serves 6–8

250 g (8 oz) orange sweet potato
250 g (8 oz) beetroot, peeled
250 g (8 oz) potato
oil, for deep-frying

1 Preheat the oven to moderate 180°C (350°F/Gas 4). Run a sharp vegetable peeler along the length of the sweet potato to create ribbons. Cut the beetroot into paper-thin slices with a sharp vegetable peeler or knife. Cut the potato into thin slices, using a mandolin slicer or knife with a crinkle-cut blade (see NOTE).
2 Fill a deep heavy-based saucepan one-third full of oil and heat until a cube of bread dropped into the oil browns in 10 seconds. Cook the vegetables in batches for about 30 seconds, or until golden and crisp. You may need to turn them with tongs or a long-handled metal spoon. Drain on paper towels and season with salt.

3 Place all the vegetable chips on a baking tray and keep warm in the oven while cooking the remaining vegetables. Serve with drinks.

NUTRITION PER SERVE (8)
Protein 2 g; Fat 5 g; Carbohydrate 12 g; Dietary Fibre 2 g; Cholesterol 0 mg; 413 kJ (99 Cal)

NOTE: If you don't have a mandolin or crinkle-cut knife at home, simply use a sharp knife to cut fine slices. The cooking time for the chips will remain the same.

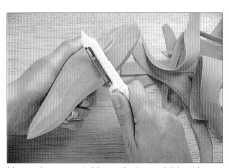

Use a sharp vegetable peeler to peel thin strips of sweet potato.

If you have a mandolin, use it for slicing the potatoes very finely.

Deep-fry the vegetables in batches until they are golden and crispy.

one-pots

TOMATO DITALINI SOUP

Preparation time: 15 minutes
Total cooking time: 20 minutes
Serves 4

2 tablespoons olive oil
1 large onion, finely chopped
2 celery sticks, finely chopped
3 vine-ripened tomatoes
1.5 litres vegetable stock
½ cup (90 g/3 oz) ditalini pasta
2 tablespoons chopped fresh
   flat-leaf parsley

1 Heat the oil in a large saucepan over medium heat. Add the onion and celery and cook for 5 minutes, or until they have softened.
2 Score a cross in the base of each tomato, then place them in a bowl of boiling water for 1 minute. Plunge into cold water and peel the skin away from the cross. Halve the tomatoes and scoop out the seeds. Roughly chop the flesh. Add the stock and tomato to the onion mixture and bring to the boil. Add the pasta and cook for 10 minutes, or until *al dente*. Season and sprinkle with parsley. Serve with crusty bread.

NUTRITION PER SERVE
Protein 8 g; Fat 11 g; Carbohydrate 23 g;
Dietary Fibre 3.5 g; Cholesterol 0 mg;
925 kJ (220 Cal)

Cook the onion and garlic until they are soft and translucent.

Halve the tomatoes horizontally and scoop out the seeds with a teaspoon.

VEGETABLE CURRY

Preparation time: 20 minutes
Total cooking time: 30 minutes
Serves 6

250 g (8 oz) potatoes, diced
250 g (8 oz) pumpkin, diced
200 g (6½ oz) cauliflower, broken
  into florets
150 g (5 oz) yellow squash, cut into
  quarters
1 tablespoon oil
2 onions, chopped
3 tablespoons curry powder
400 g (13 oz) can crushed tomatoes

1 cup (250 ml/8 fl oz) vegetable stock
150 g (5 oz) green beans, cut into
  short lengths
⅓ cup (90 g/3 oz) natural yoghurt
¼ cup (40 g/1¼ oz) sultanas

1 Bring a saucepan of water to the
boil, add the potato and pumpkin, and
cook for 6 minutes, then remove. Add
the cauliflower and squash, cook for
4 minutes, then remove.
2 Heat the oil in a large saucepan,
add the onion and cook, stirring, over
medium heat for 8 minutes, or until
starting to brown.
3 Add the curry powder and stir for
1 minute, or until fragrant. Stir in the

crushed tomato and vegetable stock.
4 Add the parboiled potato, pumpkin,
cauliflower and squash and cook for
5 minutes, then add the green beans
and cook for a further 2–3 minutes,
or until the vegetables are just tender.
5 Add the yoghurt and sultanas, and
stir to combine. Simmer for 3 minutes,
or until thickened slightly. Season to
taste and serve with lemon wedges.

NUTRITION PER SERVE
Protein 7 g; Fat 8.5 g; Carbohydrate 20 g;
Dietary Fibre 7 g; Cholesterol 2.5 mg;
805 kJ (192 Cal)

Cook the onion over medium heat until it is
starting to brown.

Add the beans and cook until the vegetables are
just tender.

Add the yoghurt and sultanas and simmer until
thickened slightly.

CHUNKY VEGETABLE SOUP

Preparation time: 25 minutes
Total cooking time: 1 hour 30 minutes
Serves 6

50 g (1¾ oz) butter
1 leek, chopped
1 celery stick, chopped
1 large carrot, chopped
1 large potato, chopped
1 parsnip, peeled and chopped
1 swede or turnip, peeled and chopped
225 g (7 oz) sweet potato, chopped

½ cup (115 g/4 oz) soup mix (see NOTE)
2 litres vegetable stock or water
1 cup (155 g/5 oz) frozen peas
125 g (4 oz) green beans, chopped
¼ cup (15 g/½ oz) chopped fresh mint
⅓ cup (20 g/¾ oz) chopped fresh parsley

1 Heat the butter in a large heavy-based pan, and cook the leek, celery, carrot, potato, parsnip, swede or turnip and sweet potato, stirring, for 5 minutes.
2 Add the soup mix and stock or water. Bring slowly to the boil, then reduce the heat and simmer, covered, for 1¼ hours, or until the soup mix has softened.
3 Add the peas and beans and cook for a further 10 minutes, or until tender. Stir in the chopped mint and parsley. Season to taste with salt and cracked black pepper. Serve hot. Delicious with crusty bread.

NUTRITION PER SERVE
Protein 3 g; Fat 7 g; Carbohydrate 15 g; Dietary Fibre 4 g; Cholesterol 20 mg; 555 kJ (135 Cal)

NOTE: Soup mix is a combination of dried beans and pulses.

Measure ½ cup (115 g/4 oz) of the soup mix before adding to the vegetables.

Top and tail the beans, then chop them into short lengths.

Add the soup mix and stock or water and slowly bring to the boil.

MIDDLE EASTERN POTATO CASSEROLE

Preparation time: 10 minutes
Total cooking time: 30 minutes
Serves 4

1/4 teaspoon saffron threads
1 kg (2 lb) potatoes, cut into large
   cubes
1 teaspoon olive oil
1 small onion, sliced
1/2 teaspoon ground turmeric
1/2 teaspoon ground coriander
1 cup (250 ml/8 fl oz) vegetable stock

1 clove garlic, crushed
1/4 cup (30 g/1 oz) raisins
1 teaspoon chopped fresh
   flat-leaf parsley
1 teaspoon chopped fresh coriander
   leaves

1 Soak the saffron in 1 tablespoon of hot water. Place the potato in a saucepan of cold, salted water. Bring to the boil and cook until tender but still firm. Drain and set aside.
2 Heat the oil in a separate saucepan, add the onion, turmeric and ground coriander and cook over low heat for 5 minutes, or until the onion is soft.

3 Add the potato, vegetable stock and garlic. Bring to the boil, then reduce the heat and simmer for 10 minutes.
4 Add the saffron with its soaking water and the raisins, and cook for 10 minutes, or until the potato is soft and the sauce has reduced and thickened. Stir in the parsley and coriander. Delicious with couscous.

NUTRITION PER SERVE
Protein 10 g; Fat 6 g; Carbohydrate 65 g;
Dietary Fibre 8 g; Cholesterol 0.5 mg;
1500 kJ (358 Cal)

Soak the saffron threads in 1 tablespoon hot water while you cook the potatoes.

Cook the onion, turmeric and ground coriander until the onion is soft.

Add the potato, stock and garlic to the saucepan and bring to the boil.

CREAM OF MUSHROOM SOUP

Preparation time: 30 minutes
Total cooking time: 15 minutes
Serves 4

500 g (1 lb) large field mushrooms
50 g (1¾ oz) butter
4 spring onions, finely chopped
3 cloves garlic, finely chopped
1 teaspoon chopped lemon thyme
2 teaspoons plain flour

1 litre (32 fl oz) vegetable stock
1 cup (250 ml/8 fl oz) cream
chives and thyme, to garnish

1 Thinly slice the mushroom caps, discarding the stalks. Melt the butter in a heavy-based pan and cook the spring onion, garlic and lemon thyme, stirring, for 1 minute, or until the garlic is golden. Add the mushroom and a good shake each of salt and white pepper. Cook for 3–4 minutes, or until the mushroom just softens. Add the flour and cook, stirring, for 1 minute.

2 Remove from the heat and add the stock, stirring continuously. Return to the heat and bring to the boil, stirring. Reduce the heat and simmer gently for 2 minutes, stirring occasionally.

3 Whisk the cream into the soup, then reheat gently, stirring. Do not allow the soup to boil. Season to taste and garnish with the chives and thyme.

NUTRITION PER SERVE
Protein 8 g; Fat 50 g; Carbohydrate 6 g;
Dietary Fibre 4 g; Cholesterol 190 mg;
1985 kJ (475 cal)

Pull the lemon thyme leaves from the stems and chop them.

Remove the stalks from the mushrooms and thinly slice the caps.

Whisk in the cream, then reheat the soup gently without boiling.

BEAN AND CAPSICUM STEW

Preparation time: 20 minutes +
  overnight soaking
Total cooking time: 1 hour 35 minutes
Serves 4–6

 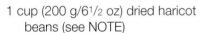

1 cup (200 g/6¹/2 oz) dried haricot
  beans (see NOTE)
2 tablespoons olive oil
2 large cloves garlic, crushed
1 red onion, halved and cut into thin
  wedges
1 red capsicum, cubed
1 green capsicum, cubed
2 x 400 g (13 oz) cans chopped
  tomatoes
2 tablespoons tomato paste
2 cups (500 ml/16 fl oz) vegetable
  stock
2 tablespoons chopped fresh basil
²/3 cup (125 g/4 oz) Kalamata olives,
  pitted
1–2 teaspoons soft brown sugar

1 Put the beans in a large bowl, cover with cold water and soak overnight. Rinse well, then transfer to a saucepan, cover with cold water and cook for 45 minutes, or until just tender. Drain.
2 Heat the oil in a large saucepan. Cook the garlic and onion over medium heat for 2–3 minutes, or until the onion is soft. Add the red and green capsicums and cook for a further 5 minutes.
3 Stir in the tomato, tomato paste, stock and beans. Simmer, covered, for 40 minutes, or until the beans are

cooked through. Stir in the basil, olives and sugar. Season with salt and pepper. Serve hot with crusty bread.

NUTRITION PER SERVE (6)
Protein 10 g; Fat 8 g; Carbohydrate 20 g;
Dietary Fibre 9.5 g; Cholesterol 0 mg;
825 kJ (197 Cal)

NOTE: 1 cup of dried haricot beans yields about 2¹/2 cups cooked beans. Use 2¹/2 cups tinned haricot or borlotti beans instead if you prefer.

Cook the garlic and onion until the onion is soft, then add the capsicum.

Simmer the stew for 40 minutes, or until the beans are cooked through.

CHICKPEA CURRY

Preparation time: 10 minutes +
  overnight soaking
Total cooking time: 1 hour 15 minutes
Serves 6

1 cup (220 g/7 oz) dried chickpeas
1 tablespoon oil
2 onions, finely chopped
2 large ripe tomatoes, chopped
1/2 teaspoon ground coriander
1 teaspoon ground cumin
1 teaspoon chilli powder
1/4 teaspoon ground turmeric
1 tablespoon channa masala
  (see NOTE)
1 small white onion, sliced
mint and coriander leaves, to garnish

1 Place the chickpeas in a bowl,
cover with water and leave to soak
overnight. Drain, rinse and place in
a large saucepan. Cover with plenty
of water and bring to the boil, then
reduce the heat and simmer for
40 minutes, or until soft. Drain.
2 Heat the oil in a large saucepan, add
the onion and cook over medium heat
for 15 minutes, or until golden brown.
Add the tomato, ground coriander and
cumin, chilli powder, turmeric and
channa masala, and 2 cups (500 ml/
16 fl oz) water and cook for 10 minutes,
or until the tomato is soft. Add the
chickpeas, season and cook for
7–10 minutes, or until the sauce
thickens. Garnish with sliced onion
and fresh mint and coriander leaves.

NUTRITION PER SERVE
Protein 8 g; Fat 9 g; Carbohydrate 17 g;
Dietary Fibre 6 g; Cholesterol 8.5 mg;
835 kJ (200 Cal)

NOTE: Channa (chole) masala is a
spice blend available at Indian grocery
stores. Garam masala can be used as
a substitute but the flavour will be a
little different.

Cook the onion over medium heat for
15 minutes, or until golden brown.

Add the soaked chickpeas and cook until the
sauce thickens.

ROASTED RED CAPSICUM SOUP

Preparation time: 50 minutes
Total cooking time: 1 hour
Serves 6
Fat per serve: 7 g

4 large red capsicums
4 ripe tomatoes
2 tablespoons oil
1 red onion, chopped
1 clove garlic, crushed
4 cups (1 litre) vegetable stock
1 teaspoon sweet chilli sauce
Parmesan and pesto, to garnish

1 Cut the capsicums into large flat pieces, removing the seeds and membrane. Place skin-side-up under a hot grill until blackened. Leave covered with a tea towel until cool, then peel away the skin and chop the flesh.
2 Score a small cross in the base of each tomato, put them in a large heatproof bowl and cover with boiling water. Leave for 1 minute, then plunge into cold water and peel the skin from the cross. Cut in half, scoop out the seeds and roughly chop the flesh.
3 Heat the oil in a large heavy-based pan and add the onion. Cook over medium heat for 10 minutes, stirring frequently, until very soft. Add the garlic and cook for a further minute. Add the capsicum, tomato and stock; bring to the boil, reduce the heat and simmer for about 20 minutes.
4 Purée the soup in a food processor or blender until smooth (in batches if necessary). Return to the pan to reheat gently and stir in the chilli sauce. Serve topped with shavings of Parmesan and a little pesto.

NUTRITION PER SERVE
Protein 3 g; Fat 7 g; Carbohydrate 5 g;
Dietary Fibre 2 g; Cholesterol 0 mg;
380 kJ (90 cal)

Once the skin of the capsicum has been blackened it should peel away easily.

Scoring a cross in the base of the tomato makes it easier to remove the skin.

Use a spoon to scoop out the seeds from the tomatoes once they have been peeled.

THREE BEAN CHILLI

Preparation time: 20 minutes +
  2 hours standing
Total cooking time: 1 hour 35 minutes
Serves 4

1 cup (220 g/7 oz) dried black beans
  (see NOTE)
2 tablespoons oil
1 large onion, finely chopped
3 cloves garlic, crushed
2 tablespoons ground cumin
1 tablespoon ground coriander
1 teaspoon ground cinnamon
1 teaspoon chilli powder
400 g (13 oz) can crushed tomatoes
1¹/2 cups (375 ml/12 fl oz) vegetable
  stock
400 g (13 oz) can chickpeas, rinsed
  and drained
400 g (13 oz) can red kidney beans,
  rinsed and drained
2 tablespoons tomato paste
1 tablespoon sugar
sour cream and corn chips, to serve

1 Place the black beans in a large pan,
cover with water and bring to the boil.
Turn off the heat and set aside for
2 hours. Drain the beans, cover with
fresh water and boil for 1 hour, until
the beans are tender but not mushy.
Drain well.
2 Heat the oil in a large pan and cook
the onion over medium-low heat for
5 minutes, until golden, stirring
frequently. Reduce the heat, add the
garlic and spices; stir for 1 minute.
3 Add the tomatoes, stock, chickpeas,
kidney beans and black beans and
combine with the onion mixture.
Bring to the boil, then simmer for
20 minutes, stirring occasionally.
4 Add the tomato paste, sugar and salt
and pepper, to taste. Simmer for a
further 5 minutes. Serve with sour
cream and corn chips on the side.

NUTRITION PER SERVE
Protein 40 g; Fat 55 g; Carbohydrate 125 g;
Dietary Fibre 36 g; Cholesterol 40 mg;
4775 kJ (1140 cal)

NOTE: If black beans are unavailable,
double the quantity of kidney beans
and chickpeas.

Do not confuse black beans with Asian black
beans, which are fermented soy.

Cook the chopped onion, stirring frequently, until
it turns golden.

Add the tomatoes, stock, chickpeas, kidney
beans and black beans to the pan.

Add salt and pepper to taste and simmer the chilli
for a further 5 minutes.

SPICED LENTIL SOUP

Preparation time: 10 minutes +
 20 minutes standing
Total cooking time: 50 minutes
Serves 4

1 eggplant
1/4 cup (60 ml/2 fl oz) olive oil
1 onion, finely chopped
2 teaspoons brown mustard seeds
2 teaspoons ground cumin
1 teaspoon garam masala
1/4 teaspoon cayenne pepper (optional)
2 large carrots, cut into cubes
1 celery stick, diced
400 g (13 oz) can crushed tomatoes

1 cup (110 g/3½ oz) puy lentils
1 litre vegetable stock
3/4 cup (35 g/1¼ oz) roughly chopped
 fresh coriander leaves
1/2 cup (125 g/4 oz) Greek-style plain
 yoghurt

1 Cut the eggplant into cubes, place in a colander, sprinkle with salt and leave for 20 minutes. Rinse well and pat dry with paper towels.
2 Heat the oil in a large saucepan over medium heat. Add the onion and cook for 5 minutes, or until soft. Add the eggplant, stir to coat in oil and cook for 3 minutes, or until softened.
3 Add all the spices and cook, stirring, for 1 minute, or until fragrant and the

mustard seeds begin to pop. Add the carrot and celery and cook for 1 minute. Stir in the tomato, lentils and stock and bring to the boil. Reduce the heat and simmer for 40 minutes, or until the lentils are tender and the liquid is reduced to a thick stew-like soup. Season to taste with salt and cracked black pepper.
4 Stir the coriander into the soup just before serving. Ladle the soup into four warmed bowls and serve with a dollop of the yoghurt on top.

NUTRITION PER SERVE
Protein 11 g; Fat 16 g; Carbohydrate 20 g;
Dietary Fibre 8.5 g; Cholesterol 5 mg;
1148 kJ (274 Cal)

Cook the chopped onion in a large saucepan until soft.

Add the spices to the vegetables and stir until fragrant.

Simmer the mixture until thick and the lentils are tender.

GREEN CURRY WITH SWEET POTATO AND EGGPLANT

Preparation time: 15 minutes
Total cooking time: 25 minutes
Serves 4–6

1 tablespoon oil
1 onion, chopped
1–2 tablespoons green curry paste
    (see NOTE)
1 eggplant, quartered and sliced
1½ cups (375 ml/12 fl oz) coconut
    milk
1 cup (250 ml/8 fl oz) vegetable stock
6 kaffir lime leaves
1 orange sweet potato, cubed
2 teaspoons soft brown sugar
2 tablespoons lime juice
2 teaspoons lime rind

1 Heat the oil in a large wok or frying pan. Add the onion and green curry paste and cook, stirring, over medium heat for 3 minutes. Add the eggplant and cook for a further 4–5 minutes, or until softened.

2 Pour in the coconut milk and vegetable stock, bring to the boil, then reduce the heat and simmer for 5 minutes. Add the kaffir lime leaves and sweet potato and cook for 10 minutes, or until the eggplant and sweet potato are very tender.

3 Mix in the sugar, lime juice and lime rind until well combined with the vegetables. Season to taste with salt and serve with steamed rice.

NUTRITION PER SERVE (6)
Protein 2.5 g; Fat 17 g; Carbohydrate 10 g;
Dietary Fibre 3 g; Cholesterol 0.5 mg;
835 kJ (200 Cal)

NOTE: Strict vegetarians should be sure to read the label and choose a green curry paste that doesn't contain shrimp paste. Alternatively, make your own curry pastes.

Eggplants are also known as aubergines. Use a sharp knife to quarter and slice the eggplant.

Stir-fry the onion and curry paste over medium heat for 3 minutes.

Cook, stirring occasionally, until the vegetables are tender.

SOBA NOODLE SOUP

Preparation time: 15 minutes +
    5 minutes standing
Total cooking time: 10 minutes
Serves 4

250 g (8 oz) packet soba noodles
2 dried shiitake mushrooms
2 litres vegetable stock
120 g (4 oz) snow peas, cut into
    thin strips
2 small carrots, cut into thin strips
2 cloves garlic, finely chopped
6 spring onions, cut into 5 cm (2 inch)
    lengths and sliced lengthways

3 cm (1 1/4 inch) piece ginger, cut into
    julienne strips
1/3 cup (80 ml/2 3/4 fl oz) soy sauce
1/4 cup (60 ml/2 fl oz) mirin or sake
1 cup (90 g/3 oz) bean sprouts
fresh coriander, to garnish

1 Cook the noodles according to
the packet instructions. Drain.
2 Soak the mushrooms in 1/2 cup
(125 ml/4 fl oz) boiling water until
soft. Drain, reserving the liquid.
Remove the stalks and finely slice
the mushrooms.
3 Combine the vegetable stock,
mushrooms, reserved liquid, snow
peas, carrot, garlic, spring onion and

ginger in a large saucepan. Bring
slowly to the boil, then reduce the
heat to low and simmer for 5 minutes,
or until the vegetables are tender. Add
the soy sauce, mirin and bean sprouts.
Cook for a further 3 minutes.
4 Divide the noodles among four
large serving bowls. Ladle the hot
liquid and vegetables over the top
and garnish with coriander.

NUTRITION PER SERVE
Protein 13 g; Fat 1.5 g; Carbohydrate 30 g;
Dietary Fibre 6 g; Cholesterol 11 mg;
1124 kJ (270 Cal)

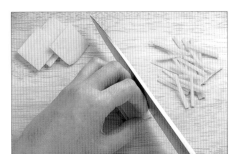

Cut the ginger into julienne strips (thin strips the size and shape of matchsticks).

After soaking the mushrooms, drain and finely slice them.

Simmer the vegetables for 5 minutes, or until they are tender.

MOROCCAN TAGINE WITH COUSCOUS

Preparation time: 20 minutes
Total cooking time: 1 hour
Serves 4–6

2 tablespoons oil
2 onions, chopped
1 teaspoon ground ginger
2 teaspoons ground paprika
2 teaspoons ground cumin
1 cinnamon stick
pinch of saffron threads
1.5 kg (3 lb) vegetables, peeled
    and cut into large chunks (carrot,
    eggplant, orange sweet potato,
    parsnip, potato, pumpkin)
1/2 preserved lemon, rinsed, pith and
    flesh removed, thinly sliced
400 g (13 oz) can peeled tomatoes
1 cup (250 ml/8 fl oz) vegetable stock
100 g (3 1/2 oz) dried pears, halved
60 g (2 oz) pitted prunes
2 zucchini, cut into large chunks
300 g (10 oz) instant couscous
1 tablespoon olive oil
3 tablespoons chopped fresh flat-leaf
    parsley
1/3 cup (50 g/1 3/4 oz) almonds

1 Preheat the oven to moderate 180°C (350°F/Gas 4). Heat the oil in a large saucepan or ovenproof dish, add the onion and cook over medium heat for 5 minutes, or until soft. Add the spices and cook for 3 minutes.
2 Add the vegetables and cook, stirring, until coated with the spices and the outside begins to soften. Add the lemon, tomatoes, stock, pears and prunes. Cover, transfer to the oven and cook for 30 minutes. Add the zucchini and cook for 15–20 minutes, or until the vegetables are tender.

3 Cover the couscous with the olive oil and 2 cups (500 ml/16 fl oz) boiling water and leave until all the water has been absorbed. Fluff with a fork.
4 Remove the cinnamon stick from the vegetables, then stir in the parsley. Serve on a large platter with the couscous formed into a ring and the

vegetable tagine in the centre, sprinkled with the almonds.

NUTRITION PER SERVE (6)
Protein 8 g; Fat 15 g; Carbohydrate 33 g;
Dietary Fibre 9 g; Cholesterol 0 mg;
1240 kJ (296 Cal)

Cook the vegetables until they are coated in spices and the outside starts to soften.

Once all the water has been absorbed, fluff the couscous with a fork.

Before serving, remove the cinnamon stick with a pair of tongs.

CHICKPEA SOUP

Preparation time: 15 minutes +
  overnight soaking
Total cooking time: 1 hour 30 minutes
Serves 4

1½ cups (330 g/11 oz) dried
  chickpeas
½ onion
1 bay leaf
½ head garlic, unpeeled (8 cloves)
2 tablespoons olive oil
1 celery stick, chopped
1 large onion, extra, finely chopped
3 cloves garlic, extra, chopped
1 teaspoon ground cumin
1 teaspoon paprika
¼ teaspoon dried chilli powder
3 teaspoons chopped fresh oregano
1 litre vegetable stock
2 tablespoons lemon juice
olive oil, extra to drizzle

1 Place the chickpeas in a bowl and cover with water. Soak overnight, then drain. Transfer the chickpeas to a saucepan and add the onion, bay leaf, garlic and 1.5 litres water. Bring to the boil, then reduce the heat and simmer for 1 hour, or until the chickpeas are tender. Drain, reserving 2 cups (500 ml/16 fl oz) cooking liquid. Discard the onion, bay leaf and garlic.
2 Heat the oil in the same saucepan, add the celery and extra onion, and cook over medium heat for 5 minutes, or until golden. Add the extra garlic and cook for a further 1 minute. Add the cumin, paprika, chilli powder and 2 teaspoons of the oregano, and cook, stirring, for 1 minute. Return the chickpeas to the pan and stir to coat with the spices.
3 Pour in the vegetable stock and reserved cooking liquid, bring to the boil, then reduce the heat and simmer for 20 minutes. Stir in the lemon juice and remaining oregano and serve drizzled with olive oil.

NUTRITION PER SERVE
Protein 16 g; Fat 20 g; Carbohydrate 34 g;
Dietary Fibre 12 g; Cholesterol 0 mg;
1565 kJ (374 Cal)

Cook the chickpeas, onion, bay leaf and garlic until the chickpeas are tender.

Add the cooked chickpeas to the pan and stir to coat in the spices.

Stir in the lemon juice and remaining fresh oregano.

COUNTRY PUMPKIN AND PASTA SOUP

Preparation time: 25 minutes
Total cooking time: 20 minutes
Serves 4–6

750 g (1½ lb) pumpkin
2 potatoes
1 tablespoon olive oil
30 g (1 oz) butter
1 large onion, finely chopped
2 cloves garlic, crushed
3 litres vegetable stock

125 g (4 oz) miniature pasta or risoni
1 tablespoon chopped fresh parsley,
  for serving

1 Peel the pumpkin and potatoes and chop into small cubes. Heat the oil and butter in a large pan. Add the onion and garlic and cook, stirring, for 5 minutes over low heat.
2 Add the pumpkin, potato and stock. Increase the heat, cover and cook for 8 minutes or until the vegetables are tender.
3 Add the pasta and cook, stirring occasionally, for 5 minutes or until the

pasta is *al dente*. Serve immediately, sprinkled with chopped parsley.

NUTRITION PER SERVE (6)
Protein 6 g; Fat 5 g; Carbohydrate 30 g; Dietary Fibre 3 g; Cholesterol 13 mg; 782 kJ (187 cal)

NOTES: Butternut or Japanese pumpkin will give this soup the sweetest flavour.

  Tiny star-shaped pasta look attractive in this soup.

Peel the pumpkin and potatoes and chop them into small cubes.

Add the pumpkin, potato and chicken stock, then cover the pan.

Add the pasta and cook, stirring occasionally, until it is *al dente*.

CURRIED LENTILS

Preparation time: 15 minutes
Total cooking time: 30 minutes
Serves 4

1 cup (250 g/8 oz) red lentils
2 cups (500 ml/16 fl oz) vegetable
  stock
1/2 teaspoon ground turmeric
50 g (1³/4 oz) ghee
1 onion, chopped
2 cloves garlic, finely chopped
1 large green chilli, seeded and finely
  chopped

2 teaspoons ground cumin
2 teaspoons ground coriander
2 tomatoes, chopped
1/2 cup (125 ml/4 fl oz) coconut milk

1 Rinse the lentils and drain well.
Place the lentils, stock and turmeric
in a large heavy-based pan. Bring to
the boil, reduce the heat and simmer,
covered, for 10 minutes, or until just
tender. Stir occasionally and check the
mixture is not catching on the bottom
of the pan.
2 Meanwhile, heat the ghee in a small
frying pan and add the onion. Cook
until soft and golden and add the

garlic, chilli, cumin and coriander.
Cook, stirring, for 2–3 minutes until
fragrant. Stir the onion and spices
into the lentil mixture and then add
the tomato. Simmer over very low
heat for 5 minutes, stirring frequently.
3 Season to taste and add the coconut
milk. Stir until heated through. Serve
with naan bread or rice.

NUTRITION PER SERVE
Protein 15 g; Fat 20 g; Carbohydrate 25 g;
Dietary Fibre 10 g; Cholesterol 35 mg;
1500 kJ (355 Cal)

Stir the lentil mixture occasionally so that it does not stick to the bottom of the pan.

Add the chopped tomato and simmer over very low heat for 5 minutes.

Season the lentils and add the coconut milk. Stir until heated through.

CREAM OF TOMATO SOUP

Preparation time: 25 minutes
Total cooking time: 30 minutes
Serves 4

1.25 kg (2¹/₂ lb) very ripe tomatoes
1 tablespoon oil
1 onion, chopped
1 clove garlic, chopped
1¹/₂ cups (375 ml/12 fl oz)
    vegetable stock
2 tablespoons tomato paste
1 teaspoon sugar
1 cup (250 ml/8 fl oz) cream

1 Score a cross in the base of each tomato. Cover with boiling water for 30 seconds, then plunge into iced water, drain and peel away the skins. Scoop out the seeds and discard, then roughly chop the flesh.

2 Heat the oil in a large pan and cook the onion for 3 minutes, or until soft. Add the garlic and cook for 1 minute longer. Add the tomato and cook for 5 minutes, stirring occasionally, until very soft. Stir in the stock, bring to the boil, reduce the heat and simmer for 10 minutes.

3 Cool slightly, then transfer to a food processor. Process in batches until smooth, and return to the pan. Add the tomato paste and sugar and bring to

the boil, stirring continuously. Reduce the heat and stir in the cream but do not allow the soup to boil. Season to taste before serving. Serve with a swirl of cream and chopped parsley.

NUTRITION PER SERVE
Protein 5 g; Fat 30 g; Carbohydrate 10 g;
Dietary Fibre 5 g; Cholesterol 85 mg;
1480 kJ (350 cal)

HINT: It is best to use plump, ripe tomatoes for this recipe.

NOTE: If you are not using home-made stock, remember to taste the soup before seasoning. Shop-bought stock can be very salty.

Plunge the tomatoes into iced water, then peel away the skin.

Cook, stirring with a wooden spoon, until the tomato is very soft.

Add the tomato paste and sugar and bring to the boil, stirring until smooth.

VEGETABLE CASSEROLE WITH HERB DUMPLINGS

Preparation time: 30 minutes
Total cooking time: 50 minutes
Serves 4

1 tablespoon olive oil
1 large onion, chopped
2 cloves garlic, crushed
2 teaspoons sweet paprika
1 large potato, chopped
1 large carrot, sliced
400 g (13 oz) can chopped tomatoes
1½ cups (375 ml/12 fl oz) vegetable
    stock
400 g (13 oz) orange sweet potato,
    cubed
150 g (5 oz) broccoli, cut into florets
2 zucchini, thickly sliced
1 cup (125 g/4 oz) self-raising flour
20 g (¾ oz) cold butter, cut into small
    cubes
2 teaspoons chopped fresh flat-leaf
    parsley
1 teaspoon fresh thyme
1 teaspoon chopped fresh rosemary
⅓ cup (80 ml/2¾ fl oz) milk
2 tablespoons light sour cream

1 Heat the oil in a large saucepan and add the onion. Cook over low heat, stirring occasionally, for 5 minutes, or until soft. Add the garlic and paprika and cook, stirring, for 1 minute, or until fragrant.
2 Add the potato, carrot, tomato and stock to the pan. Bring to the boil, then reduce the heat and simmer, covered, for 10 minutes. Add the sweet potato, broccoli and zucchini and simmer for 10 minutes, or until tender. Preheat the oven to moderately hot 200°C (400°F/Gas 6).
3 To make the dumplings, sift the flour and a pinch of salt into a bowl and add the butter. Rub the butter into the flour with your fingertips until it resembles fine breadcrumbs. Stir in the herbs and make a well in the centre. Add the milk, and mix with a flat-bladed knife, using a cutting action, until the mixture comes together in beads. Gather up the dough and lift onto a lightly floured surface, then divide into eight portions. Shape each portion into a ball.

4 Add the sour cream to the casserole. Pour into a 2 litre ovenproof dish and top with the dumplings. Bake for 20 minutes, or until the dumplings are golden and a skewer comes out clean when inserted in the centre.

NUTRITION PER SERVE
Protein 8 g; Fat 10 g; Carbohydrate 27 g; Dietary Fibre 7.5 g; Cholesterol 16 mg; 967 kJ (230 Cal)

Add the remaining vegetables and simmer for 10 minutes, or until they are tender.

Rub the butter into the flour until the mixture resembles fine breadcrumbs.

Divide the dough into eight equal portions and shape each portion into a dumpling.

PEANUT AND POTATO CURRY

Preparation time: 30 minutes
Total cooking time: 1 hour 30 minutes
Serves 4–6

3 tablespoons oil
3 cloves garlic, finely chopped
2 red chillies, finely chopped
2 teaspoons ground coriander
1 teaspoon ground cumin
1/2 teaspoon ground fenugreek seeds
pinch each of ground cinnamon and
    nutmeg

2 onions, chopped
1.5 kg (3 lb) potatoes, cubed
3/4 cup (125 g/4 oz) dry roasted
    peanuts, chopped
500 g (1 lb) ripe tomatoes, chopped
1 teaspoon soft brown sugar
2 teaspoons finely grated lime rind
2 tablespoons lime juice
coriander leaves and roughly chopped
    peanuts, to garnish

1 Heat the oil in a large, deep pan or wok and stir-fry the garlic, chilli and spices over low heat for 3 minutes, or until very fragrant. Add the onion and cook for another 3 minutes.

2 Add the potato to the pan, tossing to coat with the spice mixture. Add 1/2 cup (125 ml/4 fl oz) water, cover and cook over low heat for 10 minutes, stirring regularly.
3 Add the peanuts and tomato, uncover and simmer for 1 hour 10 minutes, stirring occasionally. Season with the sugar, rind, juice and salt and pepper. Garnish with coriander and peanuts. Serve with rice.

NUTRITION PER SERVE (6)
Protein 15 g; Fat 20 g; Carbohydrate 40 g;
Dietary Fibre 7 g; Cholesterol 0 mg;
1720 kJ (410 cal)

Stir the garlic, chilli and spices in the hot oil until very fragrant.

Use two wooden spoons to toss the potato and thoroughly coat with the spices.

Use very ripe tomatoes to give the best flavour. Add to the curry with the peanuts.

VEGETARIAN CHILLI

Preparation time: 15 minutes
Total cooking time: 40 minutes
Serves 8

3/4 cup (130 g/4¹/2 oz) burghul
   (cracked wheat)
1 tablespoon olive oil
1 large onion, finely chopped
2 cloves garlic, crushed
1 teaspoon chilli powder
2 teaspoons ground cumin
1 teaspoon cayenne pepper
¹/2 teaspoon ground cinnamon
2 x 400 g (13 oz) cans crushed tomato
3 cups (750 ml/24 fl oz) vegetable
   stock

440 g (14 oz) can red kidney beans,
   rinsed and drained
2 x 300 g (10 oz) cans chickpeas,
   rinsed and drained
310 g (10 oz) can corn kernels,
   drained
2 tablespoons tomato paste
corn chips and light sour cream,
   for serving

1 Soak the burghul in 1 cup (250 ml/
8 fl oz) of hot water for 10 minutes.
Heat the oil in a large heavy-based pan
and cook the onion for 10 minutes,
stirring often, until soft and golden.
2 Add the garlic, chilli powder, cumin,
cayenne and cinnamon and cook,
stirring, for a further minute.
3 Add the tomatoes, stock and

burghul. Bring to the boil and simmer
for 10 minutes. Stir in the beans,
chickpeas, corn and tomato paste and
simmer for 20 minutes, stirring often.
Serve with corn chips and sour cream.

NUTRITION PER SERVE
Protein 7 g; Fat 10 g; Carbohydrate 18 g;
Dietary Fibre 7 g; Cholesterol 8 mg;
780 kJ (185 Cal)

STORAGE TIME: Chilli will keep for
up to 3 days in the refrigerator and
can be frozen for up to 1 month.

Stir the garlic and spices into the pan with the
onion and cook for a minute.

Stir in the beans, chickpeas, corn kernels and
tomato paste.

Add the crushed tomatoes, stock and burghul to
the pan.

RED VEGETABLE CURRY

Preparation time: 25 minutes
Total cooking time: 20 minutes
Serves 4

225 g (7 oz) bamboo shoots or tips, drained
2 cups (500 ml/16 fl oz) coconut milk
2 tablespoons Thai red curry paste
1 onion, finely chopped
4 kaffir lime leaves
2 potatoes, roughly chopped
200 g (6¹/₂ oz) pumpkin, chopped
150 g (5 oz) green beans, chopped

1 red capsicum, chopped
3 small zucchini, chopped
2 tablespoons chopped fresh basil leaves
2 tablespoons lime juice
3 teaspoons soft brown sugar

1 Cut the bamboo shoots in half, discard the tough ends and set the shoots aside. Combine the coconut milk and curry paste in a large wok or pan with ¹/₂ cup (125 ml/4 fl oz) water. Bring to the boil, stirring occasionally.
2 Add the onion and kaffir lime leaves and allow to boil for 3 minutes.

3 Add the potato and pumpkin to the wok and cook over medium heat for 8 minutes, or until the pumpkin is nearly cooked. Add the beans, capsicum and zucchini and simmer for another 5 minutes. Add ¹/₂ cup (125 ml/4 fl oz) of water if the curry is too thick. Add the bamboo shoots and basil. Add the lime juice and sugar and taste for seasoning. Serve with steamed rice.

NUTRITION PER SERVE
Protein 7 g; Fat 26 g; Carbohydrate 22 g;
Dietary Fibre 6.5 g; Cholesterol 0 mg;
1443 kJ (345 cal)

Cut the bamboo shoots in half and discard the tough ends.

Stir in the onion and kaffir lime leaves and boil for 3 minutes.

Add the potato and pumpkin to the curry and simmer until the pumpkin is almost cooked.

SPICY VEGETABLE STEW WITH DHAL

Preparation time: 25 minutes +
  2 hours soaking
Total cooking time: 1 hour 35 minutes
Serves 4–6

DHAL
3/4 cup (165 g/5 1/2 oz) yellow split
  peas
5 cm (2 inch) piece of ginger, grated
2–3 cloves garlic, crushed
1 red chilli, seeded and chopped

3 tomatoes
2 tablespoons oil
1 teaspoon yellow mustard seeds
1 teaspoon cumin seeds
1 teaspoon ground cumin
1/2 teaspoon garam masala
1 red onion, cut into thin wedges
3 slender eggplants, thickly sliced
2 carrots, thickly sliced
1/4 cauliflower, cut into florets
1 1/2 cups (375 ml/12 fl oz) vegetable
  stock
2 small zucchini, thickly sliced
1/2 cup (90 g/3 oz) frozen peas
1/2 cup (15 g/1/2 oz) fresh coriander
  leaves

1 To make the dhal, put the split peas in a bowl, cover with water and soak for 2 hours. Drain. Place in a large saucepan with the ginger, garlic, chilli and 3 cups (750 ml/24 fl oz) water. Bring to the boil, reduce the heat and simmer for 45 minutes, or until soft.
2 Score a cross in the base of each tomato, soak in boiling water for 30 seconds, then plunge into cold water and peel the skin away from the cross. Seed and roughly chop.

3 Heat the oil in a large saucepan. Cook the spices over medium heat for 30 seconds, or until fragrant. Add the onion and cook for 2 minutes, or until the onion is soft. Stir in the tomato, eggplant, carrot and cauliflower.
4 Add the dhal and stock, mix together well and simmer, covered, for 45 minutes, or until the vegetables are

tender. Stir occasionally. Add the zucchini and peas during the last 10 minutes of cooking. Stir in the coriander leaves and serve hot.

NUTRITION PER SERVE (6)
Protein 11 g; Fat 7 g; Carbohydrate 20 g;
Dietary Fibre 8.5 g; Cholesterol 17 mg;
780 kJ (186 Cal)

Simmer the dhal for 45 minutes, or until the split peas are soft.

Score a cross in the top of each tomato, then soak in hot water to make the skin come away.

Add the dhal and stock to the stew and simmer for 45 minutes, or until the vegetables are tender.

MEDITERRANEAN VEGETABLE HOTPOT

Preparation time: 20 minutes
Total cooking time: 40 minutes
Serves 4

3 tablespoons olive oil
1 onion, chopped
2 cloves garlic, crushed
1 green capsicum, chopped
1 red capsicum, chopped
3 zucchini, sliced
3 slender eggplant, sliced
2 cups (440 g/14 oz) long-grain rice
1 cup (250 ml/8 fl oz) white wine

100 g (3¹/₂ oz) button mushrooms, sliced
3 cups (750 ml/24 fl oz) vegetable stock
400 g (13 oz) can crushed tomatoes
2 tablespoons tomato paste
150 g (5 oz) feta cheese

1 Heat the oil in a large heavy-based pan and cook the onion over medium heat for about 10 minutes, or until very soft but not browned. Add the garlic and cook for a further minute.
2 Add the green and red capsicums and cook, stirring, for 3 minutes, Add the zucchini and eggplant and sitr-fry for a further 5 minutes. Add the rice

and stir-fry for 2 minutes.
3 Add the wine, mushrooms, stock, crushed tomatoes and tomato paste. Stir to combine. Bring to the boil, reduce the heat, cover and simmer for 20 minutes. The rice should be tender. Serve immediately, topped with the crumbled feta cheese.

NUTRITION PER SERVE
Protein 20 g; Fat 25 g; Carbohydrate 92 g; Dietary Fibre 9 g; Cholesterol 25 mg; 2980 kJ (710 cal)

NOTE: Like most hotpots and casseroles, this is best made a day in advance to let the flavours develop.

Cook the onion for 10 minutes, until it is very soft but not browned.

Add the zucchini and eggplant to the pan and stir-fry for a little longer.

Add the wine, mushrooms, stock, crushed tomatoes and tomato paste.

RATATOUILLE AND PASTA SOUP

Preparation time: 25 minutes
Total cooking time: 40 minutes
Serves 6

1 medium eggplant, chopped
salt
1 tablespoon olive oil
1 large onion, chopped
1 large red capsicum, chopped
1 large green capsicum, chopped
2 cloves garlic, crushed
3 zucchini, sliced

2 x 400 g (13 oz) cans crushed
  tomatoes
1 teaspoon dried oregano leaves
1/2 teaspoon dried thyme leaves
1 litre vegetable stock
1/2 cup (45 g/1 1/2 oz) pasta spirals

1 Spread the eggplant out in a
colander and sprinkle generously with
salt. Leave for 20 minutes; rinse and
pat dry with paper towels.
2 Heat the oil in a large heavy-based
pan and cook the onion for
10 minutes, or until soft and lightly
golden. Add the capsicum, garlic,
zucchini and eggplant and cook

for 5 minutes.
3 Add the tomatoes, herbs and stock
to the pan. Bring to the boil, then
reduce the heat and simmer for
10 minutes, or until the vegetables are
tender. Add the pasta and cook for
15 minutes, until *al dente*. Serve with
Parmesan and bread.

NUTRITION PER SERVE
Protein 6 g; Fat 4 g; Carbohydrate 23 g;
Dietary Fibre 5 g; Cholesterol 0 mg;
635 kJ (150 cal)

STORAGE: This soup will keep for up
to 2 days in the refrigerator.

Put the chopped eggplant in a colander and
sprinkle generously with salt.

Add the capsicum, garlic, zucchini and eggplant
to the pan.

Once the vegetables are tender, add the pasta to
the soup.

pasta, gnocchi & rice

COTELLI WITH SPRING VEGETABLES

Preparation time: 15 minutes
Total cooking time: 20 minutes
Serves 4

500 g (1 lb) cotelli
2 cups (300 g/10 oz) frozen peas
2 cups (300 g/10 oz) frozen broad beans
1/3 cup (80 ml/2³/4 fl oz) olive oil
6 spring onions, cut into short pieces
2 cloves garlic, finely chopped
1 cup (250 ml/8 fl oz) vegetable stock
12 asparagus spears, chopped
1 lemon

1 Cook the pasta in a large pan of rapidly boiling salted water until *al dente*. Drain and return to the pan to keep warm.
2 Meanwhile, cook the peas in a saucepan of boiling water for 1–2 minutes, or until tender. Remove with a slotted spoon and plunge into cold water. Add the broad beans to the same saucepan of boiling water and cook for 1–2 minutes, then drain and plunge into cold water. Remove and slip out of their skins.
3 Heat 2 tablespoons of the oil in a frying pan. Add the spring onion and garlic and cook over medium heat for 2 minutes, or until softened. Pour in the stock and cook for 5 minutes,

or until slightly reduced. Add the asparagus and cook for 3–4 minutes, or until bright green and just tender. Stir in the peas and broad beans and cook for 2–3 minutes to heat through.
4 Toss the remaining oil through the pasta, then add the vegetable mixture, 1/2 teaspoon finely grated lemon rind and 1/4 cup (60 ml/2 fl oz) lemon juice. Season and toss together well. Serve with Parmesan shavings.

NUTRITION PER SERVE
Protein 25 g; Fat 21 g; Carbohydrate 103 g; Dietary Fibre 19 g; Cholesterol 0 mg; 2935 kJ (700 cal)

Blanch the broad beans in boiling water then iced water and then slip out of their skins.

Add the asparagus to the pan and cook until bright green and just tender.

Toss the pasta and vegetables together, then add the lemon rind and juice.

PUMPKIN AND BASIL LASAGNE

Preparation time: 20 minutes
Total cooking time: 1 hour 25 minutes
Serves 4

650 g (1 lb 5 oz) pumpkin
2 tablespoons olive oil
500 g (1 lb) ricotta cheese
1/3 cup (50 g/1 3/4 oz) pine nuts, toasted
3/4 cup (35 g/1 oz) fresh basil
2 cloves garlic, crushed
35 g (1 oz) Parmesan, grated
125 g (4 oz) fresh lasagne sheets
185 g (6 oz) mozzarella, grated

1 Preheat the oven to moderate 180°C (350°F/Gas 4). Lightly grease a baking tray. Cut the pumpkin into thin slices and arrange in a single layer on the tray. Brush with oil and cook for 1 hour, or until softened, turning halfway through cooking.
2 Place the ricotta, pine nuts, basil, garlic and Parmesan in a bowl and mix well with a wooden spoon.
3 Brush a square 20 cm (8 inch) ovenproof dish with oil. Cook the pasta according to the packet instructions. Arrange one third of the pasta sheets over the base of the dish and spread with the ricotta mixture. Top with half of the remaining lasagne sheets.

4 Arrange the pumpkin evenly over the pasta with as few gaps as possible. Season with salt and cracked black pepper and top with the final layer of pasta sheets. Sprinkle with mozzarella. Bake for 20–25 minutes, or until the cheese is golden. Leave for 10 minutes, then cut into squares.

NUTRITION PER SERVE
Protein 24 g; Fat 32 g; Carbohydrate 33 g; Dietary Fibre 4.5 g; Cholesterol 37 mg; 2166 kJ (517 Cal)

NOTE: If the pasta has no cooking instructions, blanch them one at a time until softened. Then drain and spread on tea towels to dry.

Mix together the ricotta, pine nuts, basil, garlic and Parmesan.

Cook the pasta according to the packet instructions until *al dente*.

Place the pumpkin on top of the lasagne sheet, leaving as few gaps as possible.

PASTA NAPOLITANA

Preparation time: 20 minutes
Total cooking time: 1 hour
Serves 6
Fat per serve: 7 g

1 tablespoon olive oil
1 onion, finely chopped
1 carrot, finely chopped
1 celery stick, finely chopped
500 g (1 lb) ripe tomatoes, chopped
2 tablespoons chopped fresh parsley
2 teaspoons sugar
500 g (1 lb) pasta

1 Heat the oil in a heavy-based pan. Add the onion, carrot and celery. Cover and cook for 10 minutes over low heat, stirring occasionally.

2 Add the tomato to the vegetables with the parsley, sugar and $1/2$ cup (125 ml/4 fl oz) of water. Bring to the boil, reduce the heat to low, cover and simmer for 45 minutes, stirring occasionally. Season with salt and pepper. If necessary, add a little more water to thin the sauce.

3 Add the pasta to a large pan of rapidly boiling salted water and cook until *al dente*. Drain and return to the pan. Pour the sauce over the pasta and gently toss.

NUTRITION PER SERVE
Protein 10 g; Fat 7 g; Carbohydrate 65 g; Dietary Fibre 6 g; Cholesterol 0 mg; 1540 kJ (365 cal)

Chop the vegetables into small even pieces before adding to the oil.

Add the chopped tomatoes, parsley, sugar and water to the cooked vegetables.

FETTUCINE WITH SWEET POTATO, FETA AND OLIVES

Preparation time: 15 minutes
Total cooking time: 35 minutes
Serves 6

1.5 kg (3 lb) orange sweet potato, cut into small cubes
1/3 cup (80 ml/2³/4 fl oz) olive oil
4 cloves garlic, crushed
2 tablespoons butter
4 red onions, sliced into thin wedges
500 g (1 lb) fresh basil fettucine

400 g (13 oz) soft feta cheese, diced
200 g (6¹/2 oz) small black olives
1/2 cup (30 g/1 oz) firmly packed fresh basil, torn

1 Preheat the oven to moderately hot 200°C (400°F/Gas 6). Place the sweet potato, oil and garlic in a bowl and toss to coat the sweet potato. Lay out the sweet potato in a roasting tin and roast for 15 minutes. Turn and roast for another 15 minutes, until tender and golden—make sure the sweet potato is not too soft or it will not hold its shape. Keep warm.
2 Meanwhile, melt the butter in a

deep frying pan and cook the onion over low heat, stirring occasionally, for 25–30 minutes, or until soft and slightly caramelised.
3 Cook the pasta in a large pan of rapidly boiling salted water until *al dente*. Drain and return to the pan. Add the onion to the pasta and toss together. Add the sweet potato, feta, olives and basil and gently toss. Serve drizzled with extra virgin olive oil.

NUTRITION PER SERVE
Protein 28 g; Fat 33 g; Carbohydrate 91 g;
Dietary Fibre 7 g; Cholesterol 124 mg;
3195 kJ (765 cal)

Toss the sweet potato with the flavoured oil and then roast in the oven until soft.

Cook the onion in the butter over low heat until soft and caramelised.

Toss the caramelised onion with the pasta before adding the other ingredients.

POTATO GNOCCHI WITH TOMATO AND BASIL SAUCE

Preparation time: 1 hour
Total cooking time: 50 minutes
Serves 4–6

TOMATO SAUCE
1 tablespoon oil
1 onion, chopped
1 celery stalk, chopped
2 carrots, chopped
2 x 425 g (14 oz) cans crushed
    tomatoes
1 teaspoon sugar
1/2 cup (30 g/1 oz) fresh basil,
    chopped

1 kg (2 lb) potatoes, roughly chopped
30 g (1 oz) butter
2 cups (250 g/8 oz) plain flour
2 eggs, beaten
grated Parmesan, for serving

1 To make the tomato sauce, heat the oil in a large frying pan and cook the onion, celery and carrots for 5 minutes, stirring regularly. Add the tomatoes and sugar and season. Bring to the boil, reduce the heat to very low and simmer for 20 minutes. Mix until smooth in a food processor. Add the basil leaves and set aside.

2 To make gnocchi, cook the potatoes in boiling water for 15 minutes or until very tender. Drain well and mash until smooth. Using a wooden spoon, stir in the butter and the flour, then beat in the eggs. Leave to cool.

3 Turn the potato mixture out onto a floured surface and divide in two. Roll each half into a long sausage shape. Cut into 3–4 cm (1¼–1½ inch) pieces and press each piece with the back of a fork to give the gnocchi ridges.

4 Bring a large pan of water to the boil, add the gnocchi and cook for 3 minutes, or until they rise to the surface. Drain with a slotted spoon and serve with the tomato sauce and grated Parmesan cheese.

NUTRITION PER SERVE (6)
Protein 15 g; Fat 10 g; Carbohydrate 60 g;
Dietary Fibre 5 g; Cholesterol 75 mg;
1680 kJ (400 cal)

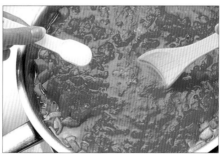

Add the tomatoes, sugar and seasoning to the frying vegetables.

Use a wooden spoon to beat the eggs into the mashed potato.

Press each piece of gnocchi with the back of a fork to give the traditional ridges.

Cook the gnocchi in boiling water until they rise to the surface, then drain.

VEGETARIAN PAELLA

Preparation time: 20 minutes +
  overnight soaking
Total cooking time: 40 minutes
Serves 6

1 cup (200 g/6½ oz) dried haricot
  beans
¼ teaspoon saffron threads
2 tablespoons olive oil
1 onion, diced
1 red capsicum, cut into
  1 cm x 4 cm (½ inch x 1½ inch)
  strips
5 cloves garlic, crushed
1¼ cups (275 g/9 oz) paella rice or
  arborio
1 tablespoon sweet paprika
½ teaspoon mixed spice
3 cups (750 ml/24 fl oz) vegetable
  stock
400 g (13 oz) can diced tomatoes
1½ tablespoons tomato paste
1 cup (150 g/5 oz) fresh or frozen soy
  beans
100 g (3½ oz) silverbeet leaves
  (no stems), shredded
400 g (13 oz) can artichoke hearts,
  drained and quartered
4 tablespoons chopped fresh
  coriander leaves

1 Place the haricot beans in a large bowl, cover with cold water and soak overnight. Drain and rinse well.
2 Place the saffron threads in a small frying pan over medium–low heat. Dry-fry, shaking the pan, for 1 minute, or until darkened. Remove from the heat and when cool, crumble into a small bowl. Pour in ½ cup (125 ml) warm water and allow to steep.
3 Heat the oil in a paella or frying pan. Add the onion and capsicum and cook over medium–high heat for 4 minutes, or until the onion softens. Stir in the garlic and cook for 1 minute. Reduce the heat and add the beans, rice, paprika, mixed spice and ½ teaspoon salt. Stir to coat. Add the saffron water, stock, tomatoes and tomato paste and bring to the boil. Cover, reduce the heat and simmer for 20 minutes.
4 Stir in the soy beans, silverbeet and artichoke hearts and cook, covered, for 8 minutes, or until all the liquid is absorbed and the rice and beans are tender. Turn off the heat and leave for 5 minutes. Stir in the coriander just before serving.

NUTRITION PER SERVE
Protein 16 g; Fat 8 g; Carbohydrate 55 g; Dietary Fibre 12 g; Cholesterol 0 mg; 1510 kJ (360 Cal)

Allow the crumbled saffron threads to steep in warm water.

Add the haricot beans, rice, paprika, mixed spice and salt and stir to coat.

RED LENTIL AND RICOTTA LASAGNE

Preparation time: 30 minutes + soaking
Total cooking time: 2 hours 10 minutes
Serves 6

1/2 cup (125 g/4 oz) red lentils
2 teaspoons olive oil
2–3 cloves garlic, crushed
1 large onion, chopped
1 small red capsicum, chopped
2 zucchini, sliced
1 celery stick, sliced
2 x 425 g (14 oz) cans chopped
   tomatoes
2 tablespoons tomato paste
1 teaspoon dried oregano
350 g (12 oz) ricotta
12 dried or fresh lasagne sheets
60 g (2 oz) reduced-fat Cheddar,
   grated

WHITE SAUCE
1/3 cup (40 g/1 1/4 oz) cornflour
3 cups (750 ml/24 fl oz) skim milk
1/4 onion
1/2 teaspoon ground nutmeg

1 Soak the lentils in boiling water to cover for at least 30 minutes, then drain. Meanwhile, heat the oil in a large pan, add the garlic and onion and cook for 2 minutes. Add the capsicum, zucchini and celery and cook for 2–3 minutes.

2 Add the lentils, tomato, tomato paste, oregano and 1 1/2 cups (375 ml/12 fl oz) water. Bring slowly to the boil, reduce the heat and simmer for 30 minutes, or until the lentils are tender. Stir occasionally.

3 To make the white sauce, blend the cornflour with 2 tablespoons of the milk in a pan until smooth. Pour the remaining milk into the pan, add the onion and stir over low heat until the mixture boils and thickens. Add the nutmeg and season with pepper, then cook over low heat for 5 minutes. Remove the onion.

4 Beat the ricotta with about 1/2 cup (125 ml/4 fl oz) of the white sauce. Preheat the oven to moderate 180°C (350°F/Gas 4). Spread one-third of the lentil mixture over the base of a 3-litre capacity ovenproof dish. Cover with a layer of lasagne sheets. Spread another third of the lentil mixture over the pasta, then spread the ricotta evenly over the top. Follow with another layer of lasagne, then the remaining lentils. Pour the white sauce evenly over the top and sprinkle with the grated cheese. Bake for 1 hour, covering loosely with foil if the top starts to brown too much. Leave to stand for 5 minutes before cutting.

NUTRITION PER SERVE
Protein 25 g; Fat 10 g; Carbohydrate 65 g; Dietary Fibre 9 g; Cholesterol 40 mg; 1995 kJ (475 Cal)

Chop the onion and capsicum into quite small pieces and slice the zucchini.

Build up layers of the lentil mixture, lasagne sheets and ricotta.

Pour the white sauce evenly over the top of the lasagne, then sprinkle with cheese.

FETTUCINE WITH CREAMY SPINACH AND ROAST TOMATO

Preparation time: 10 minutes
Total cooking time: 35 minutes
Serves 4–6

6 Roma tomatoes
2 tablespoons butter
2 cloves garlic, crushed
1 onion, chopped
500 g (1 lb) English spinach
1 cup (250 ml/8 fl oz) vegetable stock
1/2 cup (125 ml/4 fl oz) thick cream
500 g (1 lb) fresh spinach fettucine
60 g (2 oz) shaved Parmesan

1 Preheat the oven to hot 220°C (425°F/Gas 7). Cut the tomatoes in half lengthways, then cut each half into three wedges. Place the wedges on a lightly greased baking tray and bake for 30–35 minutes, or until softened and slightly golden. Meanwhile, heat the butter in a large frying pan. Add the garlic and onion and cook over medium heat for 5 minutes, or until the onion is soft. Add the spinach, stock and cream, increase the heat to high and bring to the boil. Simmer rapidly for 5 minutes then season well and process in a food processor until smooth.

2 Meanwhile, cook the pasta in a large pan of rapidly boiling salted water until *al dente*. Drain and return to the pan to keep warm. Toss with the spinach sauce. Divide among serving bowls and top with the roasted tomatoes and Parmesan shavings.

NUTRITION PER SERVE (6)
Protein 17 g; Fat 18 g; Carbohydrate 65 g; Dietary Fibre 8 g; Cholesterol 49 mg; 2035 kJ (485 cal)

Add the spinach, stock and cream to the sauce and simmer rapidly.

Transfer the spinach sauce to a food processor and mix until smooth.

LINGUINE WITH RED PEPPER SAUCE

Preparation time: 20 minutes
Total cooking time: 30 minutes
Serves 4–6

3 red capsicums
3 tablespoons olive oil
1 large onion, sliced
2 cloves garlic, crushed
1/4–1/2 teaspoon chilli flakes or powder
1/2 cup (125 ml/4 fl oz) cream
2 tablespoons chopped fresh oregano
500 g (1 lb) linguine or spaghetti

1 Halve each capsicum, removing the membrane and seeds and cut into large pieces. Place skin-side-up under a hot grill and cook for 8 minutes or until black and blistered. Cover with a damp tea towel and allow to cool. Peel off the skin and cut the capsicum into thin strips.
2 Heat the oil in a large heavy-based pan. Add the onion and cook, stirring, over low heat for 8 minutes or until soft. Add the capsicum, garlic, chilli and cream and cook for 2 minutes, stirring occasionally. Add salt and pepper and the oregano.
3 Meanwhile, cook the pasta in a large pan of rapidly boiling salted water until *al dente*. Drain and return to the pan to keep warm. Add the sauce to the pasta and toss well before serving.

NUTRITION PER SERVE (6)
Protein 11 g; Fat 20 g; Carbohydrate 62 g;
Dietary Fibre 5 g; Cholesterol 62 mg;
1970 kJ (470 cal)

HINT: If you use dried oregano use about one-third of the quantity as dried herbs are stronger in flavour.
VARIATION: For a stronger capsicum flavour, omit the cream.

Add the capsicum, garlic, chilli and cream and cook for 2 minutes.

Grill the capsicum until the skin is blackened and will peel away easily.

Cook the pasta in a large pan of boiling salted water until it is tender.

ZUCCHINI PASTA BAKE

Preparation time: 15 minutes
Total cooking time: 40 minutes
Serves 4

200 g (6½ oz) risoni
40 g (1¼ oz) butter
4 spring onions, thinly sliced
400 g (13 oz) zucchini, grated
4 eggs
½ cup (125 ml/4 fl oz) cream
100 g (3½ oz) ricotta (see NOTE)
⅔ cup (100 g/3½ oz) grated
   mozzarella
¾ cup (75 g/2½ oz) grated Parmesan

1 Preheat the oven to moderate 180°C
(350°F/Gas 4). Cook the pasta in a
large saucepan of boiling water until
al dente. Drain well. Meanwhile, heat
the butter in a frying pan, add the
spring onion and cook for 1 minute,
then add the zucchini and cook for
a further 4 minutes, or until soft.
Cool slightly.
2 Place the eggs, cream, ricotta,
mozzarella, risoni and half of the
Parmesan in a bowl and mix together
well. Stir in the zucchini mixture, then
season with salt and pepper. Spoon
the mixture into four 2 cup (500 ml/
16 fl oz) greased ovenproof dishes,
but do not fill to the brim. Sprinkle
with the remaining Parmesan and
cook for 25–30 minutes, or until
firm and golden.

NUTRITION PER SERVE
Protein 28.5 g; Fat 40.5 g; Carbohydrate 39 g;
Dietary Fibre 4.5 g; Cholesterol 310.5 mg;
2635 kJ (630 Cal)

NOTE: With such simple flavours, it
is important to use good-quality fresh
ricotta from the delicatessen or the
deli section of your local supermarket.

Cook the grated zucchini until it is soft, taking care
not to burn it.

Spoon the mixture into four ovenproof dishes.
Take care to not fill them to the top.

GREEN PILAU WITH CASHEWS

Preparation time: 15 minutes
Total cooking time: 1 hour 10 minutes
Serves 6

200 g (6½ oz) baby English spinach
²/₃ cup (100 g/3½ oz) cashew nuts, chopped
2 tablespoons olive oil
6 spring onions, chopped
1½ cups (300 g/10 oz) long-grain brown rice
2 cloves garlic, finely chopped
1 teaspoon fennel seeds
2 tablespoons lemon juice
2½ cups (600 ml/20 fl oz) vegetable stock
3 tablespoons chopped fresh mint
3 tablespoons chopped fresh flat-leaf parsley

1 Preheat the oven to moderate 180°C (350°F/Gas 4). Shred the English spinach leaves.
2 Place the cashew nuts on a baking tray and roast for 5–10 minutes, or until golden brown—watch carefully.
3 Heat the oil in a large frying pan and cook the spring onion over medium heat for 2 minutes, or until soft. Add the rice, garlic and fennel seeds and cook, stirring frequently, for 1–2 minutes, or until the rice is evenly coated. Increase the heat to high, add the lemon juice, stock and 1 teaspoon salt and bring to the boil. Reduce to low, cover and cook for 45 minutes without lifting the lid.
4 Remove from the heat and sprinkle with the spinach and herbs. Leave, covered, for 8 minutes, then fork the spinach and herbs through the rice. Season. Serve sprinkled with cashews.

NUTRITION PER SERVE
Protein 6 g; Fat 12 g; Carbohydrate 32 g; Dietary Fibre 3.5 g; Cholesterol 0 mg; 1091 kJ (260 Cal)

Wash the spinach thoroughly, trim away any stalks and shred the leaves.

Stir the rice until it is evenly coated and starts to stick to the pan.

Fork the spinach and herbs through the rice and sprinkle with cashews to serve.

FREE-FORM WILD MUSHROOM LASAGNE

Preparation time: 10 minutes +
  15 minutes soaking
Total cooking time: 15 minutes
Serves 4

10 g (¹/₄ oz) dried porcini mushrooms
350 g (11 oz) wild mushrooms
  (e.g. shiitake, oyster, Swiss brown)
30 g (1 oz) butter
1 small onion, halved and thinly sliced
1 tablespoon chopped fresh thyme
3 egg yolks
¹/₂ cup (125 ml/4 fl oz) thick cream
1 cup (100 g/3¹/₂ oz) grated
  Parmesan
8 fresh lasagne sheets (10 x 25 cm/
  4 x 10 inches)

1 Soak the porcini in ¹/₄ cup (60 ml/ 2 fl oz) boiling water for 15 minutes. Strain through a sieve, reserving the liquid. Cut the larger of all the mushrooms in half. Heat the butter in a frying pan and cook the onion over medium heat for 1–2 minutes, or until just soft. Add the thyme and mushrooms (including the porcini) and cook for 1–2 minutes, or until softened. Pour in the reserved mushroom liquid and cook for 1–2 minutes, or until the liquid has evaporated. Set aside.

2 Beat the egg yolks, cream and half the Parmesan in a large bowl. Cook the lasagne sheets in a large saucepan of boiling water for 2–3 minutes, stirring gently. Drain well and toss the sheets gently through the egg mixture while hot. Reheat the mushrooms quickly. To serve, place a sheet of folded lasagne on a plate, top with some mushrooms, then another sheet of folded lasagne. Drizzle with any remaining egg mixture and sprinkle with the remaining Parmesan.

NUTRITION PER SERVE
Protein 20 g; Fat 30 g; Carbohydrate 30 g;
Dietary Fibre 4.5 g; Cholesterol 213 mg;
1950 kJ (465 cal)

Add the thyme and all the mushrooms to the pan, then add the porcini soaking liquid.

Toss the lasagne sheets gently through the egg, cream and Parmesan mixture.

BUCATINI WITH EGGPLANT AND MUSHROOMS

Preparation time: 20 minutes
Total cooking time: 25 minutes
Serves 4–6

2 tablespoons olive oil
250 g (8 oz) mushrooms, sliced
1 eggplant, diced
2 cloves garlic, crushed

825 g (1 lb 11 oz) can tomatoes
500 g (1 lb) bucatini or spaghetti
1/4 cup (15 g/1/2 oz) chopped fresh
  parsley

1 Heat the oil in a pan and cook the mushrooms, eggplant and garlic, stirring, for 4 minutes. Add the tomatoes, cover and simmer for 15 minutes.
2 Meanwhile, cook the pasta in a large pan of rapidly boiling salted water until *al dente*. Drain and return to the pan to keep warm. Season the sauce and stir in the parsley. Toss with the pasta and serve immediately.

NUTRITION PER SERVE (6)
Protein 12 g; Fat 8 g; Carbohydrate 65 g;
Dietary Fibre 8 g; Cholesterol 0 mg;
1600 kJ (383 cal)

HINT: If the pasta is cooked before you are ready to serve you can prevent it sticking together by tossing it with a little olive oil after draining.

Wipe the mushrooms clean and slice them. Cut the eggplant into small cubes.

Heat the oil in a pan and cook the mushrooms, eggplant and garlic.

Add the chopped parsley to the sauce just before tossing with the pasta.

ROAST PUMPKIN SAUCE ON PAPPARDELLE

Preparation time: 15 minutes
Total cooking time: 35 minutes
Serves 4

1.5 kg (3 lb) butternut pumpkin, cut into small cubes
4 cloves garlic, crushed
3 teaspoons fresh thyme leaves
100 ml (3 1/2 fl oz) olive oil
500 g (1 lb) pappardelle
2 tablespoons cream
3/4 cup (185 ml/6 fl oz) hot vegetable stock
30 g (1 oz) shaved Parmesan

1 Preheat the oven to moderately hot 200°C (400°F/Gas 6). Place the pumpkin, garlic, thyme and 1/4 cup (60 ml/2 fl oz) of the olive oil in a bowl and toss together. Season with salt, transfer to a baking tray and cook for 30 minutes, or until tender and golden. Meanwhile, cook the pasta in a large pan of rapidly boiling salted water until *al dente*. Drain and return to the pan. Toss through the remaining oil and keep warm.

2 Place the pumpkin and cream in a food processor or blender and process until smooth. Add the hot stock and process until smooth. Season with salt and cracked black pepper and gently toss through the pasta. Serve with Parmesan and extra thyme leaves.

NUTRITION PER SERVE
Protein 26 g; Fat 30 g; Carbohydrate 110 g; Dietary Fibre 8 g; Cholesterol 43 mg; 3400 kJ (810 cal)

NOTE: The sauce becomes thick on standing, so serve immediately.

Toss the pumpkin through the herbs and oil, then season with salt and roast until soft.

Put the cooked pumpkin and cream in a food processor and mix until smooth.

83

PASTA PRIMAVERA

Preparation time: 25 minutes
Total cooking time: 10–15 minutes
Serves 4

500 g (1 lb) pasta (see NOTE)
1 cup (155 g/5 oz) frozen broad beans
200 g (6¹/₂ oz) sugar snap peas
155 g (5 oz) asparagus spears
30 g (1 oz) butter
1 cup (250 ml/8 fl oz) cream
60 g (2 oz) freshly grated Parmesan

1 Cook the pasta in a large pan of rapidly boiling salted water until *al dente*. Drain and return to the pan to keep warm.
2 Cook the beans in a pan of boiling water for 2 minutes. Plunge them into iced water and then drain. Remove and discard the skins from the broad beans—you can usually just squeeze them out, otherwise carefully slit the skins first.
3 Trim the stalks from the peas and break the woody ends from the asparagus spears. Cut the asparagus into short lengths.
4 Melt the butter in a heavy-based frying pan. Add the vegetables, cream and Parmesan. Simmer gently over medium heat for 3–4 minutes, or until the peas and asparagus are bright green and just tender. Season with some salt and pepper. Pour the sauce over the warm pasta and toss to combine. Serve immediately.

NUTRITION PER SERVE
Protein 30 g; Fat 35 g; Carbohydrate 95 g; Dietary Fibre 12 g; Cholesterol 105 mg; 3420 kJ (815 cal)

NOTE: Traditionally, primavera is served with spaghetti. Here it is shown with spaghettini, a thin spaghetti.

After cooking, the broad beans should slip easily out of their skins.

Trim the stalks from the sugar snap peas and snap the woody ends from the asparagus.

ASIAN MUSHROOM RISOTTO

Preparation time: 20 minutes +
    20 minutes soaking
Total cooking time: 45 minutes
Serves 4

10 g (¹/₄ oz) dried Chinese
    mushrooms
2 cups (500 ml/16 fl oz) vegetable
    stock
2 tablespoons soy sauce
¹/₃ cup (80 ml/2³/₄ fl oz) mirin
150 g (5 oz) Swiss brown mushrooms
150 g (5 oz) oyster mushrooms
100 g (3¹/₂ oz) fresh shiitake
    mushrooms
150 g (5 oz) shimeji mushrooms
1 tablespoon butter
1 tablespoon olive oil
1 onion, finely chopped
3 cloves garlic, crushed
1 tablespoon finely chopped fresh
    ginger
2 cups (440 g/14 oz) arborio rice
100 g (3¹/₂ oz) enoki mushrooms,
    trimmed
2 tablespoons snipped fresh chives
shaved Parmesan, to garnish

1 Put the Chinese mushrooms in a bowl, cover with 2¹/₂ cups (625 ml/ 20 fl oz) hot water and soak for 20 minutes, then drain, reserving the liquid. Remove the stems and thinly slice the caps.
2 Heat the vegetable stock, soy sauce, mirin, reserved mushroom liquid and 1 cup (250 ml/8 fl oz) water in a large saucepan. Bring to the boil, then keep at a low simmer, skimming off any scum that forms on the surface.
3 Trim and slice the Swiss brown, oyster and shiitake mushrooms, discarding any woody ends. Trim the shimeji and pull apart into small clumps. Melt the butter in a large saucepan over medium heat, add all the mushrooms except the Chinese and enoki and cook, stirring, for 3 minutes, or until wilted, then remove from the pan.
4 Add the oil to the pan, then add the chopped onion and cook, stirring, for 4–5 minutes, or until soft and just starting to brown. Add the garlic and

ginger and stir well until fragrant. Add the rice and stir for 1 minute, or until it is well coated in the oil mixture.
5 Gradually add ¹/₂ cup (125 ml/ 4 fl oz) of the hot stock to the rice. Stir constantly over medium heat until nearly all the liquid has been absorbed. Continue adding more stock, a little at a time, stirring for 20–25 minutes, until all the stock has

been absorbed and the rice is tender.
6 Add all the mushrooms and stir well. Season and garnish with the chives and shaved Parmesan.

NUTRITION PER SERVE
Protein 17 g; Fat 15 g; Carbohydrate 92 g;
Dietary Fibre 8 g; Cholesterol 28 mg;
2397 kJ (573 Cal)

Divide the shimeji and slice the Swiss brown, oyster and shiitake mushrooms.

Stir the rice constantly until nearly all the liquid has been absorbed.

FOUR-CHEESE MACARONI

Preparation time: 15 minutes
Total cooking time: 40 minutes
Serves 4

450 g (14 oz) elbow macaroni
2 tablespoons butter
300 ml (10 fl oz) cream
125 g (4 oz) fontina cheese, sliced
125 g (4 oz) provolone cheese, grated
100 g (3¹/₂ oz) Gruyère cheese, grated
125 g (4 oz) blue castello cheese, crumbled
¹/₂ cup (40 g/1¹/₄ oz) fresh white breadcrumbs
¹/₄ cup (30 g/1 oz) grated Parmesan

1 Preheat the oven to moderate 180°C (350°F/Gas 4). Cook the pasta in a large pan of rapidly boiling salted water until *al dente*. Drain well and return to the pan to keep warm. Melt half the butter in a large saucepan. Add the cream and, when just coming to the boil, add the fontina, provolone, Gruyère and blue castello cheeses, stirring constantly over low heat for 3 minutes, or until melted. Season with salt and white pepper. Add the pasta to the cheese mixture and mix well.
2 Spoon the mixture into a lightly greased shallow 2-litre ovenproof dish. Sprinkle with the breadcrumbs mixed with the Parmesan, dot with the remaining cubed butter and bake for 25 minutes, or until the top is golden and crisp.

NUTRITION PER SERVE
Protein 49 g; Fat 81 g; Carbohydrate 89 g;
Dietary Fibre 6 g; Cholesterol 260 mg;
5330 kJ (1275 cal)

When the cream is just coming to the boil, add the four cheeses and stir until melted.

Add the pasta to the cheese sauce and then spoon into the dish.

BEETROOT RAVIOLI WITH SAGE BURNT BUTTER

Preparation time: 15 minutes
Total cooking time: 15 minutes
Serves 4

340 g (11 oz) jar baby beetroots in
    sweet vinegar
40 g (1¼ oz) grated Parmesan
250 g (8 oz) ricotta
750 g (1½ lb) fresh lasagne sheets
fine cornmeal, for sprinkling
200 g (6½ oz) butter, chopped
8 fresh sage leaves, torn
2 cloves garlic, crushed

1 Drain the beetroot, then grate it into a bowl. Add the Parmesan and ricotta and mix well. Lay a sheet of pasta on a flat surface and place evenly spaced tablespoons of the ricotta mixture on the pasta to give 12 mounds—four across and three down. Flatten the mounds slightly. Lightly brush the edges of the pasta sheet and around each pile of filling with water.

2 Place a second sheet of pasta over the top and gently press around each mound to seal and enclose the filling. Using a pasta wheel or sharp knife, cut the pasta into 12 ravioli. Lay them out separately on a lined tray that has been sprinkled with the cornmeal. Repeat with the remaining filling and

lasagne sheets to make 24 ravioli. Gently remove any excess air bubbles after cutting so that they are completely sealed.

3 Cook the pasta in a large pan of rapidly boiling salted water until *al dente*. Drain and return to the pan to keep warm. Melt the butter in a saucepan and cook for 3–4 minutes, or until golden brown. Remove from the heat, stir in the sage and garlic and spoon over the ravioli. Sprinkle with shaved Parmesan to serve.

NUTRITION PER SERVE
Protein 16 g; Fat 52 g; Carbohydrate 33 g;
Dietary Fibre 3 g; Cholesterol 168 mg;
2720 kJ (650 cal)

Brush between the mounds of filling with a little water so the pasta will stick.

Use a pasta wheel or sharp knife to cut the pasta into 12 ravioli.

Remove the melted butter from the heat and stir in the sage and garlic.

PENNE WITH MUSHROOM AND HERB SAUCE

Preparation time: 15 minutes
Total cooking time: 25 minutes
Serves 4

2 tablespoons olive oil
500 g (1 lb) button mushrooms, sliced
2 cloves garlic, crushed
2 teaspoons chopped fresh marjoram
1/2 cup (125 ml/4 fl oz) dry white white
1/3 cup (80 ml/2³/4 fl oz) light cream
375 g (12 oz) penne

1 tablespoon lemon juice
1 teaspoon finely grated lemon rind
2 tablespoons chopped fresh parsley
1/2 cup (60 g/2 oz) grated Parmesan

1 Heat the oil in a large heavy-based frying pan over high heat. Add the mushrooms and cook for 3 minutes, stirring constantly. Add the garlic and marjoram and cook for 2 minutes.
2 Add the dry white wine, reduce the heat and simmer for 5 minutes, or until nearly all the liquid has evaporated. Stir in the cream and continue to cook over low heat for 5 minutes, or until

the sauce has thickened.
3 Meanwhile, cook the pasta in a large pan of rapidly boiling salted water until *al dente*. Drain and return to the pan to keep warm.
4 Add the lemon juice, rind, parsley and half the Parmesan to the sauce. Season to taste. Toss the penne through the sauce and sprinkle with the remaining Parmesan.

NUTRITION PER SERVE
Protein 20 g; Fat 18 g; Carbohydrate 67 g;
Dietary Fibre 6.5 g; Cholesterol 25 mg;
2275 kJ (545 cal)

Add the garlic and marjoram to the softened mushrooms and cook for another 2 minutes.

Cook the pasta in a large saucepan of boiling water until *al dente*.

Stir the lemon juice, rind, parsley and half the Parmesan into the sauce.

INDIVIDUAL SPINACH AND LEEK LASAGNES

Preparation time: 20 minutes
Total cooking time: 45 minutes
Serves 4

8 fresh lasagne sheets
8 Roma tomatoes, halved
4 large field mushrooms, stalks
    removed
1/3 cup (80 ml/2³/4 fl oz) olive oil
1 tablespoon chopped fresh thyme
60 g (2 oz) butter
2 large leeks, finely sliced
2 cloves garlic, crushed
500 g (1 lb) packet frozen chopped
    English spinach, thawed
1 cup (250 g/8 oz) light sour cream
1 cup (250 g/8 oz) light cream
600 g (1¹/4 lb) ricotta
1 egg, lightly beaten
1 cup (125 g/4 oz) grated Cheddar

1 Preheat the oven to moderately hot 200°C (400°F/Gas 6). Lightly grease four 2-cup (500 ml/16 fl oz) ovenproof dishes. Cut half the lasagne sheets to fit the bases of the dishes.
2 Place the tomatoes and mushrooms face down in a baking dish. Mix together the oil and thyme and drizzle over the tomato and mushroom. Season. Bake for 15 minutes, then turn over and bake for another 10 minutes, or until softened. Roughly chop.
3 Heat the butter in a frying pan, add the leek and garlic and cook over medium heat for 2–3 minutes, or until soft. Squeeze the liquid from the spinach and add to the leek mixture with the sour cream and cream. Stir well, bring to the boil and cook for 5 minutes, or until reduced slightly. Stir in the tomato and mushroom.
4 Spoon half the spinach and leek mixture into the dishes. Cover with the remaining lasagne sheets and repeat with the remaining mixture. Spread with the combined ricotta and egg and sprinkle with Cheddar. Bake for 20 minutes, or until golden.

NUTRITION PER SERVE
Protein 60 g; Fat 20 g; Carbohydrate 60 g;
Dietary Fibre 23 g; Cholesterol 435 mg;
5833 kJ (1393 cal)

Cut the lasagne sheets to fit the bases of the prepared dishes.

Drizzle the tomato and mushrooms with the oil and thyme and bake until soft.

Stir the spinach, sour cream and cream into the leek mixture.

Cover with another piece of lasagne and repeat with the remaining mixture.

chargrills, pan-fries & stir-fries

VEGETARIAN BURGERS WITH CORIANDER GARLIC CREAM

Preparation time: 30 minutes
Total cooking time: 20 minutes
Makes 10 burgers

1 cup (250 g/8 oz) red lentils
1 tablespoon oil
2 onions, sliced
1 tablespoon tandoori mix powder
425 g (14 oz) can chickpeas, drained
1 tablespoon grated fresh ginger
1 egg
3 tablespoons chopped fresh parsley
2 tablespoons chopped fresh
    coriander
2¼ cups (180 g/6 oz) fresh
    breadcrumbs
plain flour, for dusting

CORIANDER GARLIC CREAM
½ cup (125 g/4 oz) sour cream
½ cup (125 ml/4 fl oz) cream
1 clove garlic, crushed
2 tablespoons chopped fresh
    coriander
2 tablespoons chopped fresh parsley

1 Simmer the lentils in a large pan of water for 8 minutes or until tender. Drain well. Heat the oil in a pan and cook the onion until tender. Add the tandoori mix and stir until fragrant.
2 Put the chickpeas, half the lentils, the ginger, egg and onion mixture in a food processor. Process for 20 seconds or until smooth. Transfer to a bowl. Stir in the remaining lentils, parsley, coriander and breadcrumbs.
3 Divide into 10 portions and shape into burgers. (If the mixture is too soft, refrigerate for 15 minutes to firm.) Toss the burgers in flour and place on a hot,

lightly oiled barbecue grill or flatplate. Cook for 3–4 minutes each side or until browned.
4 For the coriander garlic cream, mix together the sour cream, cream, garlic and herbs. Serve with the burgers.

NUTRITION PER BURGER
Protein 11 g; Fat 14 g; Carbohydrate 26 g;
Dietary Fibre 5 g; Cholesterol 50 mg;
1155 kJ (276 cal)

STORAGE: The burgers can be prepared up to 2 days in advance and stored, covered, in the fridge. The cream can be stored, covered, in the fridge for up to 3 days.

NOTE: The coriander garlic cream is also delicious with chicken or fish burgers.

Heat the oil in a pan and cook the onion until tender, then add the tandoori mix.

Process the chickpea mixture, then transfer to a bowl and mix with the other ingredients.

Shape the portions into burgers and then toss in flour, shaking off the excess, before cooking.

TOFU KEBABS WITH MISO PESTO

Preparation time: 30 minutes +
  1 hour marinating
Total cooking time: 10 minutes
Serves 4

1 large red capsicum, cubed
12 button mushrooms, halved
6 pickling onions, quartered
3 zucchini, cut into chunks
450 g (14 oz) firm tofu, cubed
1/2 cup (125 ml/4 fl oz) light olive oil
3 tablespoons light soy sauce
2 cloves garlic, crushed
2 teaspoons grated fresh ginger

MISO PESTO
1/2 cup (90 g/3 oz) unsalted roasted
  peanuts
2 cups (60 g/2 oz) firmly packed fresh
  coriander leaves
2 tablespoons white miso paste
2 cloves garlic
100 ml (31/2 oz) olive oil

1 If using wooden skewers, soak them in water for 30 minutes to prevent scorching. Thread the vegetables and tofu alternately onto 12 skewers, then place in a large non-metallic dish.

2 Mix together the olive oil, soy sauce, garlic and ginger, then pour half over the kebabs. Cover and leave to marinate for 1 hour.

3 To make the miso pesto, finely chop the peanuts, coriander leaves, miso paste and garlic in a food processor. Slowly add the olive oil while the machine is still running and blend to a smooth paste.

4 Cook the kebabs on a hot, lightly oiled barbecue flatplate or grill, turning and brushing with the remaining marinade, for 4–6 minutes, or until the edges are slightly brown. Serve with the miso pesto.

NUTRITION PER SERVE
Protein 8 g; Fat 64 g; Carbohydrate 10 g;
Dietary Fibre 4 g; Cholesterol 0 mg;
2698 kJ (645 cal)

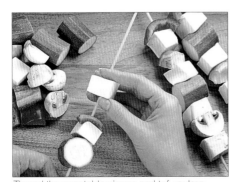

Thread the vegetable pieces and tofu cubes alternately onto the skewers.

Mix the nuts, coriander leaves, miso and garlic in a food processor until finely chopped.

Brush the kebabs with the remaining marinade during cooking.

SPICY BROCCOLI AND CAULIFLOWER

Preparation time: 15 minutes
Total cooking time: 10 minutes
Serves 4

1 teaspoon ground cumin
1 teaspoon ground coriander
2 tablespoons oil
2 cloves garlic, crushed
1 teaspoon grated fresh ginger
1/2 teaspoon chilli powder

1 onion, cut into wedges
200 g (6 1/2 oz) cauliflower, cut into
   bite-sized florets
200 g (6 1/2 oz) broccoli, cut into bite-
   sized florets
200 g (6 1/2 oz) haloumi cheese, diced
1 tablespoon lemon juice

1 Heat the wok until very hot, add the cumin and coriander, and dry-fry the spices for 1 minute. Add the oil with the garlic, ginger and chilli powder, and stir-fry briefly. Add the onion and cook for 2–3 minutes, being careful not to burn the spices.

2 Add the cauliflower and broccoli, and stir-fry until they are cooked through but still crisp. Add the haloumi and toss well until the haloumi is coated with the spices and is just beginning to melt. Season well and serve sprinkled with lemon juice.

NUTRITION PER SERVE
Protein 12 g; Fat 15 g; Carbohydrate 3 g;
Dietary Fibre 4 g; Cholesterol 20 mg;
820 kJ (195 cal)

Haloumi cheese comes in a block—cut it into small cubes.

Dry-fry the ground cumin and coriander in a very hot wok.

Add the onion wedges to the spice mixture and toss to coat.

94

TEMPEH STIR-FRY

Preparation time: 15 minutes
Total cooking time: 15 minutes
Serves 4

1 teaspoon sesame oil
1 tablespoon peanut oil
2 cloves garlic, crushed
1 tablespoon grated fresh ginger
1 red chilli, finely sliced
4 spring onions, sliced on the diagonal
300 g (10 oz) tempeh, diced
500 g (1 lb) baby bok choy leaves
800 g (1 lb 10 oz) Chinese broccoli, chopped
1/2 cup (125 ml/4 fl oz) mushroom oyster sauce
2 tablespoons rice vinegar
2 tablespoons fresh coriander leaves
3 tablespoons toasted cashew nuts

1 Heat the oils in a wok over high heat, add the garlic, ginger, chilli and spring onion and cook for 1–2 minutes, or until the onion is soft. Add the tempeh and cook for 5 minutes, or until golden. Remove and keep warm.

2 Add half the greens and 1 tablespoon water to the wok and cook, covered, for 3–4 minutes, or until wilted. Remove and repeat with the remaining greens and more water.

3 Return the greens and tempeh to the wok, add the sauce and vinegar and warm through. Top with the coriander and nuts. Serve with rice.

NUTRITION PER SERVE
Protein 23 g; Fat 15 g; Carbohydrate 12 g; Dietary Fibre 15 g; Cholesterol 0 mg; 2220 kJ (529 Cal)

Stir-fry the garlic, ginger, chilli and spring onion for 1–2 minutes.

Add the tempeh to the wok and stir-fry for 5 minutes, or until golden.

Add the greens to the wok in two batches and cook until wilted.

ASPARAGUS STIR-FRIED WITH MUSTARD

Preparation time: 10 minutes
Total cooking time: 10 minutes
Serves 2

480 g (15 oz) asparagus
1 tablespoon oil
1 red onion, sliced
1 clove garlic, crushed
1 tablespoon wholegrain mustard
1 teaspoon honey
1/2 cup (125 ml/4 fl oz) cream

1 Break the woody ends off the asparagus by holding both ends of the spear and bending gently until it snaps at its natural breaking point. Cut the asparagus into 5 cm (2 inch) lengths.
2 Heat the wok until very hot, add the oil and swirl to coat the side. Stir-fry the onion for 2–3 minutes, or until tender. Stir in the crushed garlic and cook for 1 minute. Add the asparagus to the wok and stir-fry for 3–4 minutes, or until tender, being careful not to overcook the asparagus.
3 Remove the asparagus from the wok, set it aside and keep it warm. Combine the wholegrain mustard, honey and cream. Add to the wok and bring to the boil, then reduce the heat and simmer for 2–3 minutes, or until the mixture reduces and thickens slightly. Return the asparagus to the wok and toss it through the cream mixture. Serve immediately.

NUTRITION PER SERVE
Protein 8.5 g; Fat 35 g; Carbohydrate 10 g;
Dietary Fibre 5 g; Cholesterol 85 mg;
1685 kJ (405 Cal)

VARIATION: When asparagus is in season, white and purple asparagus are also available. Vary the recipe by using a mixture of the three colours. Do not overcook the purple asparagus or it will turn green as it cooks.

HINT: This dish can also be served on croutons, toasted ciabatta or toasted wholegrain bread as a smart starter or first course.

Gently bend the asparagus spear and the tough woody end will naturally snap off.

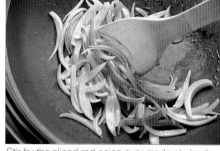

Stir-fry the sliced red onion over moderate heat for 2–3 minutes, or until tender.

VEGETARIAN PHAD THAI

Preparation time: 20 minutes
Total cooking time: 15 minutes
Serves 4

400 g (13 oz) flat rice-stick noodles
2 tablespoons peanut oil
2 eggs, lightly beaten
1 onion, cut into thin wedges
2 cloves garlic, crushed
1 small red capsicum, thinly sliced
100 g (3¹/₂ oz) deep-fried tofu puffs, cut into thin strips
6 spring onions, thinly sliced
¹/₂ cup (30 g/1 oz) chopped fresh coriander leaves

¹/₄ cup (60 ml/2 fl oz) soy sauce
2 tablespoons lime juice
1 tablespoon soft brown sugar
2 teaspoons sambal oelek
1 cup (90 g/3 oz) bean shoots
3 tablespoons chopped roasted unsalted peanuts

1 Cook the noodles in a saucepan of boiling water for 5–10 minutes, or until tender. Drain and set aside.
2 Heat a wok over high heat and add enough peanut oil to coat the bottom and side. When smoking, add the egg and swirl to form a thin omelette. Cook for 30 seconds, or until just set. Roll up, remove and thinly slice.
3 Heat the remaining oil in the wok.

Add the onion, garlic and capsicum and cook over high heat for 2–3 minutes, or until the onion softens. Add the noodles, tossing well. Stir in the omelette, tofu, spring onion and half the coriander.
4 Pour in the combined soy sauce, lime juice, sugar and sambal oelek, then toss to coat the noodles. Sprinkle with the bean shoots and top with roasted peanuts and the remaining coriander. Serve immediately.

NUTRITION PER SERVE
Protein 13 g; Fat 21 g; Carbohydrate 34 g;
Dietary Fibre 5 g; Cholesterol 90 mg;
1565 kJ (375 Cal)

Buy deep-fried tofu puffs (rather than silken or firm tofu) and cut into thin strips.

Cook the egg, swirling the wok, to make a thin omelette, then roll up and thinly slice.

Stir in the omelette, tofu, spring onion and fresh coriander.

PUY LENTILS AND BEAN PUREE ON MUSHROOMS WITH RED WINE SAUCE

Preparation time: 30 minutes
Total cooking time: 35 minutes
Serves 4

4 large (10 cm/4 inch) field
    mushrooms
1 tablespoon olive oil
1 red onion, cut into thin wedges
1 clove garlic, crushed
1 cup (200 g/6^1/$_2$ oz) puy lentils
^{3}/$_4$ cup (185 ml/6 fl oz) red wine
1^3/$_4$ cups (440 ml/14 fl oz) vegetable
    stock
1 tablespoon finely chopped fresh flat-
    leaf parsley
30 g (1 oz) butter
2 cloves garlic, crushed, extra

BEAN PUREE
1 large potato, cut into chunks
2 tablespoons extra virgin olive oil
400 g (13 oz) can cannellini beans,
    drained and rinsed
2 large cloves garlic, crushed
1 tablespoon vegetable stock

RED WINE SAUCE
^{2}/$_3$ cup (170 ml/5^1/$_2$ fl oz) red wine
2 tablespoons tomato paste
1^1/$_2$ cups (375 ml/12 fl oz) vegetable
    stock
1 tablespoon soft brown sugar

1 Remove the stalks from the mushrooms and chop them. Heat the oil in a large saucepan and cook the onion over medium heat for 2–3 minutes, or until soft. Add the garlic and mushroom stalks and cook for a further 1 minute. Stir in the lentils, wine and stock and bring to the boil. Reduce the heat and simmer, covered, for 20–25 minutes, stirring occasionally, or until reduced and the lentils are cooked through. If the mixture is too wet, remove the lid and boil until slightly thick. Stir in the parsley and keep warm.

2 Meanwhile, to make the bean purée, bring a small saucepan of water to the boil over high heat and cook the potato for 10 minutes, or until tender. Drain and mash with a potato masher or fork until smooth. Stir in half the extra virgin olive oil. Combine the cannellini beans and garlic in a food processor bowl. Add the stock and the remaining oil and process until smooth. Transfer to a bowl and fold in the mashed potato. Keep warm.

3 Melt the butter in a deep frying pan. Add the mushrooms and extra garlic and cook in batches over medium heat for 4 minutes each side, or until tender. Remove and keep warm.

4 To make the red wine sauce, add the red wine to the same frying pan, then scrape the bottom to remove any sediment. Add the combined tomato paste, stock and sugar and bring to the boil. Cook for about 10 minutes, or until reduced and thickened.

5 To assemble, place the mushrooms onto serving plates and top with the bean purée. Spoon on the lentil mixture and drizzle with the red wine sauce. Season and serve immediately.

NUTRITION PER SERVE
Protein 23 g; Fat 23 g; Carbohydrate 42 g;
Dietary Fibre 17 g; Cholesterol 20 mg;
2198 kJ (525 cal)

NOTE: The mushrooms tend to shrivel if you keep them warm in the oven—either turn the oven off or find another warm place.

Remove the stalks from the field mushrooms and finely chop them.

Simmer the lentils until they are cooked through and the liquid is reduced.

Fold the mashed potato into the purée of cannellini beans and garlic.

Fry the mushrooms over medium heat until they are tender, turning once.

Scrape the bottom of the frying pan to stir in any sediment stuck to the pan.

Cook the red wine sauce for 10 minutes, until it is reduced and thickened.

TOFU WITH CARROT AND GINGER SAUCE

Preparation time: 25 minutes +
  overnight marinating
Total cooking time: 30 minutes
Serves 6

2 x 300 g (10 oz) packets firm tofu
1/2 cup (125 ml/4 fl oz) freshly
  squeezed orange juice
1 tablespoon soft brown sugar
1 tablespoon soy sauce
2 tablespoons chopped fresh
  coriander leaves
2 cloves garlic, crushed
1 teaspoon grated fresh ginger
2–3 tablespoons oil
1 kg (2 lb) baby bok choy, cut into
  quarters lengthways

CARROT AND GINGER SAUCE
300 g (10 oz) carrots, chopped
2 teaspoons grated fresh ginger
2/3 cup (170 ml/5 1/2 fl oz) orange juice
1/2 cup (125 ml/4 fl oz) vegetable
  stock

1 Drain the tofu, then slice each block into six lengthways. Place in a single layer in a flat non-metallic dish. Mix the juice, sugar, soy sauce, coriander, garlic and ginger in a jug, then pour over the tofu. Cover and refrigerate overnight, turning once.

2 Drain the tofu, reserving the marinade. Heat the oil in a large frying pan and cook the tofu in batches over high heat for 2–3 minutes each side, or until golden. Remove and keep warm. Bring the marinade to the boil in a saucepan, then reduce the heat and simmer for 1 minute. Remove from the heat and keep warm.

3 Heat a wok, add the bok choy and 1 tablespoon water and cook, covered, over medium heat for 2–3 minutes, or until tender. Remove and keep warm.

4 Put all the sauce ingredients in a saucepan, bring to the boil, then reduce the heat and simmer, covered, for 5–6 minutes, or until the carrot is tender. Transfer to a food processor and blend until smooth.

5 To serve, divide the bok choy among six plates. Top with some sauce, then the tofu and drizzle on a little of the marinade before serving.

NUTRITION PER SERVE
Protein 14 g; Fat 14 g; Carbohydrate 14 g;
Dietary Fibre 8.5 g; Cholesterol 0 mg;
1034 kJ (246 cal)

Use a non-metallic dish for marinating in acidic liquids such as orange juice.

Cook the tofu slices in batches until golden brown on both sides.

Blend the carrot and ginger sauce in a food processor until smooth.

TAMARI ROASTED ALMONDS WITH SPICY GREEN BEANS

Preparation time: 10 minutes
Total cooking time: 25 minutes
Serves 4–6

1 tablespoon sesame oil
2¹/2 cups (500 g/1 lb) jasmine rice
2 tablespoons sesame oil, extra
1 long red chilli, seeded and finely chopped
2 cm (³/4 inch) piece of fresh ginger, peeled and grated
2 cloves garlic, crushed
375 g (12 oz) green beans, cut into short lengths
¹/2 cup (125 ml/4 fl oz) hoisin sauce
1 tablespoon soft brown sugar
2 tablespoons mirin
250 g (8 oz) tamari roasted almonds, roughly chopped (see NOTE)

1 Preheat the oven to moderately hot 200°C (400°F/Gas 6). Heat the oil in a 1.5 litre ovenproof dish. Add the rice and stir to coat with oil. Stir in 1 litre boiling water. Cover and bake for 20 minutes, or until all the water is absorbed. Keep warm.
2 Meanwhile, heat the extra oil in a wok or large frying pan and cook the chilli, ginger and garlic for 1 minute, or until lightly browned. Add the beans, hoisin sauce and sugar and stir-fry for 2 minutes. Stir in the mirin and cook for 1 minute, or until the beans are tender but still crunchy.
3 Remove from the heat and stir in the almonds. Serve on a bed of the rice.

NUTRITION PER SERVE (6)
Protein 15 g; Fat 34 g; Carbohydrate 80 g;
Dietary Fibre 9.5 g; Cholesterol 0 mg;
2874 kJ (687 Cal)

NOTE: Tamari roasted almonds are available from health-food stores.

When chopping chillies, it's a good idea to wear rubber gloves to prevent chilli burns.

Cook the rice in the oven until all the water has been absorbed.

Stir-fry the beans for 2 minutes, tossing to coat them in the sauce.

CHILLI NOODLE AND NUT STIR-FRY

Preparation time: 20 minutes
Total cooking time: 12 minutes
Serves 4

1½ tablespoons oil
1 tablespoon sesame oil
2–3 small red chillies, finely chopped
1 large onion, cut into thin wedges
4 cloves garlic, very thinly sliced
1 red capsicum, cut into strips
1 green capsicum, cut into strips
2 large carrots, cut into batons
100 g (3½ oz) green beans
2 celery sticks, cut into batons

2 teaspoons honey
500 g (1 lb) Hokkien noodles, gently separated
100 g (3½ oz) dry-roasted peanuts
100 g (3½ oz) honey-roasted cashews
¼ cup (30 g/1 oz) chopped garlic chives, or 4 spring onions, chopped
sweet chilli sauce and sesame oil, to serve

1 Heat the wok over low heat, add the oils and swirl them to coat the side. When the oil is warm, add the chilli and heat until the oil is very hot.
2 Add the onion and garlic, and stir-fry for 1 minute, or until the onion just softens. Add the capsicum, carrot and beans, and stir-fry for 1 minute. Add the celery, honey and 1 tablespoon water, and season with salt and pepper. Toss well, then cover and cook for 1–2 minutes, or until the vegetables are just tender.
3 Add the noodles and nuts and toss well. Cook, covered, for 1–2 minutes, or until the noodles are heated through. Stir in the garlic chives and serve, drizzled with the sweet chilli sauce and sesame oil.

NUTRITION PER SERVE
Protein 20 g; Fat 45 g; Carbohydrate 75 g; Dietary Fibre 7 g; Cholesterol 0 mg; 3330 kJ (795 cal)

Peel the cloves of garlic, then cut them into paper-thin slices.

Remove the seeds from the capsicum and cut the flesh into strips.

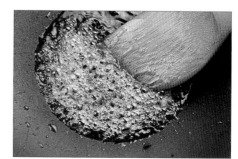
Heat the oil until warm, then add the chilli and heat until the oil is very hot.

TOFU BURGERS

Preparation time: 25 minutes +
  30 minutes refrigeration
Total cooking time: 30 minutes
Serves 6

1 tablespoon olive oil
1 red onion, finely chopped
200 g (6½ oz) Swiss brown
  mushrooms, finely chopped
350 g (11 oz) hard tofu (see NOTE)
2 large cloves garlic
3 tablespoons chopped fresh basil
2 cups (200 g/6½ oz) dry wholemeal
  breadcrumbs
1 egg, lightly beaten
2 tablespoons balsamic vinegar
2 tablespoons sweet chilli sauce
1½ cups (150 g/5 oz) dry wholemeal
  breadcrumbs, extra
olive oil, for shallow-frying
6 wholemeal or wholegrain bread rolls
½ cup (125 g/4 oz) mayonnaise
100 g (3½ oz) semi-dried tomatoes
60 g (2 oz) rocket leaves
sweet chilli sauce, to serve

1 Heat the oil in a frying pan and cook the onion over medium heat for 2–3 minutes, or until soft. Add the mushrooms and cook for a further 2 minutes. Cool slightly.
2 Blend 250 g (8 oz) of the tofu with the garlic and basil in a food processor until smooth. Transfer to a large bowl and stir in the onion mixture, breadcrumbs, egg, vinegar and sweet chilli sauce. Grate the remaining tofu and fold through the mixture, then refrigerate for 30 minutes. Divide the mixture into six and form into patties, pressing together well. Coat them in the extra breadcrumbs.
3 Heat 1 cm (½ inch) oil in a deep frying pan and cook the patties in two batches for 4–5 minutes each side, or until golden. Turn carefully to prevent them breaking up. Drain on crumpled paper towels and season with salt.
4 Halve the bread rolls and toast under a hot grill. Spread mayonnaise over both sides of each roll. Layer semi-dried tomatoes, a tofu patty and rocket leaves in each roll and drizzle with sweet chilli sauce.

NUTRITION PER SERVE
Protein 23 g; Fat 24 g; Carbohydrate 86 g;
Dietary Fibre 10 g; Cholesterol 37 mg;
2740 kJ (653 Cal)

NOTE: Hard tofu (not to be confused with 'firm' tofu) is quite rubbery and firm and won't break up during cooking. It's perfect for patties, stir-frying and pan-frying.

Mix the tofu, garlic and basil in a food processor until smooth.

Grate the remaining hard tofu and fold it into the mixture. Refrigerate for 30 minutes.

Be careful when you turn the patties during frying. You don't want them to break up.

VEGETABLE AND TOFU KEBABS

Preparation time: 40 minutes +
  30 minutes marinating
Total cooking time: 30 minutes
Serves 4

500 g (1 lb) firm tofu, cubed
1 red capsicum, cubed
3 zucchini, thickly sliced
4 small onions, cut into quarters
300 g (10 oz) button mushrooms, cut
  into quarters
1/2 cup (125 ml/4 fl oz) tamari
1/2 cup (125 ml/4 fl oz) sesame oil
2.5 cm (1 inch) piece fresh ginger,
  peeled and grated
1/2 cup (180 g/6 oz) honey
1 tablespoon sesame oil, extra
1 small onion, finely chopped
1 clove garlic, crushed
2 teaspoons chilli paste
1 cup (250 g/8 oz) smooth peanut
  butter
1 cup (250 ml/8 fl oz) coconut milk
1 tablespoon soft brown sugar
1 tablespoon tamari
1 tablespoon lemon juice
3 tablespoons peanuts, roasted and
  chopped
3 tablespoons sesame seeds, toasted

1 Preheat the oven to hot 220°C (425°F/Gas 7). Soak 12 bamboo skewers in water to prevent scorching. Thread the tofu, capsicum, zucchini, onions and mushrooms onto the skewers. Arrange in a shallow, non-metallic dish.
2 Combine the tamari, oil, ginger and honey and pour over the kebabs. Leave for 30 minutes.
3 To make the peanut sauce, heat the extra oil in a large frying pan over medium heat and cook the onion, garlic and chilli paste for 1–2 minutes, or until the onion is soft. Reduce the heat, add the peanut butter, coconut milk, sugar, tamari and lemon juice and stir. Bring to the boil, then reduce the heat and simmer for 10 minutes, or until just thick. Stir in the peanuts. If the sauce is too thick, add water.
4 Cook the kebabs on a hot, lightly oiled barbecue grill or flatplate, basting with the marinade and turning occasionally, for 10–15 minutes, or until tender. Drizzle peanut sauce over the kebabs and sprinkle with sesame seeds to serve.

NUTRITION PER SERVE
Protein 31.5 g; Fat 65 g; Carbohydrate 25.5 g;
Dietary Fibre 15 g; Cholesterol 0 mg;
3334 kJ (795 cal)

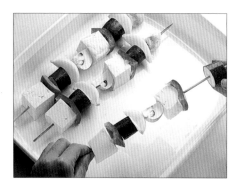

Thread alternating pieces of tofu and vegetables onto the skewers.

Simmer the peanut sauce for 10 minutes, or until just thickened.

Cook the skewers, occasionally turning and basting with the marinade.

SESAME TOFU STIR-FRY

Preparation time: 20 minutes +
  30 minutes marinating
Total cooking time: 10 minutes
Serves 4

300 g (10 oz) firm tofu
2 teaspoons sesame oil
2 tablespoons soy sauce
1 tablespoon sesame seeds
2 tablespoons oil
3 zucchini, sliced
150 g (5 oz) button mushrooms,
  halved or quartered
1 large red capsicum, cut into squares
2 cloves garlic, crushed
3 cups (550 g/1 lb 2 oz) cold, cooked
  brown rice
1–2 tablespoons soy sauce, extra

1 Drain the tofu and pat dry with paper towels. Cut into cubes, place in a glass or ceramic bowl and add the sesame oil and soy sauce. Stir well and leave in the fridge to marinate for 30 minutes, stirring occasionally.
2 Heat the wok until very hot, add the sesame seeds and dry-fry until lightly golden. Tip onto a plate to cool.
3 Reheat the wok, add the oil and swirl it around to coat the side. Remove the tofu from the dish with a slotted spoon and reserve the marinade. Stir-fry the tofu over high heat, turning occasionally, for about 3 minutes, or until browned. Remove from the wok and set aside.
4 Add the vegetables and garlic, and cook, stirring often, until they are just tender. Add the rice and tofu, and stir-fry until heated through.

5 Add the toasted sesame seeds, the reserved marinade and extra soy sauce to taste. Toss to coat the tofu and vegetables, then serve immediately.

NUTRITION PER SERVE
Protein 15 g; Fat 20 g; Carbohydrate 50 g;
Dietary Fibre 5.5 g; Cholesterol 0 mg;
1815 kJ (435 cal)

Dry-fry the sesame seeds until they are lightly golden brown.

VEGETABLE PLATTER

Preparation time: 25 minutes
Total cooking time: 1 hour
Serves 8

HERB VINAIGRETTE
1/2 cup (125 ml/4 fl oz) olive oil
2 tablespoons balsamic vinegar
2 cloves garlic, crushed
2 tablespoons fresh lime juice
1/3 cup (20 g/3/4 oz) chopped fresh
    mint, basil and coriander, mixed

4 potatoes, unpeeled and halved
400 g (13 oz) pumpkin, unpeeled, cut
    into large pieces
300 g (10 oz) sweet potatoes,
    unpeeled and cut into large pieces
4 slender eggplants, halved
2 red onions, cut into wedges
1 yellow capsicum, quartered
1 red capsicum, quartered
1 green capsicum, quartered
8 large flat mushrooms, trimmed

BASIL MAYONNAISE
4 egg yolks
2 teaspoons mustard
1/4 cup (60 ml/2 fl oz) lemon juice
1 2/3 cups (410 ml/13 fl oz) olive oil
1/3 cup (20 g/3/4 oz) fresh basil leaves

1 To make the herb vinaigrette, whisk together the ingredients. Brush over the potato, pumpkin and sweet potato and wrap in foil. Cook on a hot, lightly oiled barbecue grill for 40–50 minutes, or until tender.
2 Brush the eggplant, onion, capsicum and mushrooms with the vinaigrette. Place on the barbecue for 10 minutes, or until golden brown.
3 To make the mayonnaise, process the yolks, mustard and lemon juice in a food processor for 1 minute, or until pale and creamy. Slowly add the oil with the motor running. When thick, add the basil and mix for 20 seconds.
4 Drizzle the vegetables with the remaining vinaigrette and serve with the mayonnaise.

NUTRITION PER SERVE
Protein 5 g; Fat 65 g; Carbohydrate 15 g;
Dietary Fibre 5 g; Cholesterol 90 mg;
2840 kJ (675 cal)

Cut the pumpkin, sweet potato, capsicum and onion into large pieces.

Brush the potato, pumpkin and sweet potato with vinaigrette and wrap in foil.

Barbecue the eggplant, onion, capsicum and mushrooms on a grill.

Add the basil to the mayonnaise and process for 20 seconds.

STIR-FRIED CRISP TOFU IN A HOT BEAN SAUCE

Preparation time: 35 minutes +
  30 minutes marinating
Total cooking time: 15 minutes
Serves 4

500 g (1 lb) firm tofu, cut into
    small cubes
2 tablespoons peanut oil
1/4 cup (60 ml/2 fl oz) soy sauce
2 teaspoons finely grated fresh ginger
3/4 cup (125 g/4 oz) rice flour
oil, for cooking
2 onions, cut into thin wedges
2 cloves garlic, finely chopped
2 teaspoons soft brown sugar
1/2 red capsicum, cut into short,
    thin strips
5 spring onions, cut into short pieces
2 tablespoons dry sherry
2 teaspoons finely grated orange rind
2 tablespoons hot bean paste

1 Place the tofu in a glass or ceramic bowl with the peanut oil. Add the soy sauce and ginger, cover and refrigerate for 30 minutes.
2 Drain the tofu, reserving the marinade, and toss several pieces at a time in the rice flour to coat heavily. Heat the wok until very hot, add about 1/4 cup (60 ml/2 fl oz) of the oil and swirl it around to coat the side. Add the tofu to the hot oil and stir-fry over medium heat for 1 1/2 minutes, or until golden all over. Remove from the wok and drain on paper towels. Repeat with the remaining tofu. Keep warm. Drain any oil from the wok.
3 Reheat the wok and stir-fry the onion, garlic and sugar for 3 minutes, or until golden. Add the capsicum,

spring onion, sherry, orange rind, bean paste and the reserved tofu marinade. Stir and bring to the boil. Return the tofu to the wok, toss to heat through, and serve.

NUTRITION PER SERVE
Protein 15 g; Fat 8 g; Carbohydrate 40 g;
Dietary Fibre 3 g; Cholesterol 0 mg;
1215 kJ (290 Cal)

Marinate the tofu in the peanut oil and soy sauce for 30 minutes before cooking.

Drain the tofu in a sieve, then toss it in the rice flour to coat heavily.

Stir-fry the tofu until it is golden on all sides, then drain on paper towels.

VEGETABLES PROVENCALE

Preparation time: 25 minutes
Total cooking time: 30 minutes
Serves 4

1 large eggplant, cut into thick
   batons
3/4 cup (90 g/3 oz) plain flour
oil, for cooking
2 onions, cut into wedges
2 cloves garlic, finely chopped
1/2 cup (125 ml/4 fl oz) white wine
150 g (5 oz) green beans
4 large zucchini, sliced

200 g (6 1/2 oz) button mushrooms
1/4 cup (15 g/1/2 oz) chopped basil
2 tomatoes, chopped
2 tablespoons tomato paste

1 Toss the eggplant in the flour until it
is lightly coated. Heat the wok until
very hot, add about 2 tablespoons of
the oil and swirl it around to coat the
side. Stir-fry the eggplant in three or
four batches over medium-high heat,
tossing regularly for about 3 minutes,
or until it is golden and just cooked.
Add more oil to the wok with each
batch. Remove from the wok and
drain on paper towels. Season with
salt and freshly ground black pepper.

2 Add the onion and garlic to the wok
and stir-fry for 3 minutes, or until
softened. Add the wine, beans and
zucchini. Cook for 2 minutes, tossing
regularly. Add the mushrooms and
cook, covered, for 2 minutes. Stir in
the basil, tomato and tomato paste.
Cook for 1 minute, then season well
with salt and pepper.
3 Arrange the tomato mixture on a
plate, top with the eggplant and serve.

NUTRITION PER SERVE
Protein 9 g; Fat 6 g; Carbohydrate 25 g;
Dietary Fibre 8.5 g; Cholesterol 0 mg;
910 kJ (215 cal)

Trim the top of the eggplant and cut the eggplant
into short, thick batons.

Use two spoons to toss the eggplant in the flour
until it is lightly coated.

Stir-fry the floured eggplant in batches until it is
golden and just cooked.

PUMPKIN AND CASHEW STIR-FRY

Preparation time: 20 minutes
Total cooking time: 15 minutes
Serves 4–6

oil, for cooking
1 cup (155 g/5 oz) raw cashew nuts
1 leek, white part only, sliced
2 teaspoons ground coriander
2 teaspoons ground cumin
2 teaspoons brown mustard seeds
2 cloves garlic, crushed

1 kg (2 lb) butternut pumpkin, cubed
3/4 cup (185 ml/6 fl oz) orange juice
1 teaspoon soft brown sugar

1 Heat the wok until very hot, add 1 tablespoon of the oil and swirl to coat. Stir-fry the cashews until golden, then drain on paper towels. Stir-fry the leek for 2–3 minutes, or until softened. Remove from the wok.
2 Reheat the wok, add 1 tablespoon of the oil and stir-fry the coriander, cumin, mustard seeds and garlic for 2 minutes, or until the spices are fragrant and the mustard seeds begin to pop. Add the pumpkin and stir to coat well. Stir-fry for 5 minutes, or until the pumpkin is brown and tender.
3 Add the orange juice and sugar. Bring to the boil and cook for 5 minutes. Add the leek and three-quarters of the cashews and toss well. Top with the remaining cashews to serve.

NUTRITION PER SERVE (6)
Protein 8 g; Fat 20 g; Carbohydrate 20 g; Dietary Fibre 4 g; Cholesterol 0 mg; 1240 kJ (295 cal)

Stir-fry the cashews in 1 tablespoon of the oil until they are golden.

Reheat the wok and stir-fry the coriander, cumin, mustard seeds and garlic.

Add the pumpkin and stir to coat well in the spices. Stir-fry until brown and tender.

from the oven

STUFFED EGGPLANTS

Preparation time: 20 minutes
Total cooking time: 1 hour
Serves 4
Fat per serve: 10 g

1/3 cup (60 g/2 oz) brown lentils
2 large eggplants
cooking oil spray
1 red onion, chopped
2 cloves garlic, crushed
1 red capsicum, finely chopped
1/4 cup (40 g/11/4 oz) pine nuts, toasted
3/4 cup (140 g/41/2 oz) cooked short-grain rice

440 g (14 oz) can chopped tomatoes
2 tablespoons chopped fresh coriander
1 tablespoon chopped fresh parsley
2 tablespoons grated Parmesan

1 Simmer the brown lentils in a pan of water for 25 minutes, or until soft; drain. Slice the eggplants in half lengthways and scoop out the flesh, leaving a 1 cm (1/2 inch) shell. Chop the flesh finely.
2 Spray a deep, large non-stick frying pan with oil, add 1 tablespoon water to the pan, then add the onion and garlic and stir until softened. Add the cooked lentils to the pan with the capsicum, pine nuts, rice, tomato and eggplant flesh. Stir over medium heat for 10 minutes, or until the eggplant has softened. Add the fresh coriander and parsley. Season, then toss until well mixed.
3 Cook the eggplant shells in boiling water for 4–5 minutes, or until tender, or microwave on High (100%) for 8 minutes. Spoon the filling into the eggplant shells and sprinkle with the Parmesan. Grill for 5–10 minutes, or until golden. Serve immediately.

NUTRITION PER SERVE
Protein 15 g; Fat 10 g; Carbohydrate 50 g;
Dietary Fibre 8.5 g; Cholesterol 9.5 mg;
1490 kJ (355 cal)

Scoop out the flesh, leaving a shell on the inside of the eggplant halves.

Stir in the chopped fresh coriander and parsley and season.

Cook the eggplant halves in boiling water for about 5 minutes, or until tender.

ROASTED TOMATO AND GARLIC TART

Preparation time: 40 minutes
Total cooking time: 1 hour 10 minutes
Serves 4

4 Roma tomatoes, halved
1 tablespoon olive oil
1 teaspoon balsamic vinegar
1 teaspoon salt
5–10 cloves garlic, unpeeled
2 sheets puff pastry
1 egg, lightly beaten
10 bocconcini, halved
small fresh basil leaves, to garnish

1 Preheat the oven to 200°C (400°F/ Gas 6). Put the tomatoes, cut-side-up, on a baking tray and drizzle with the olive oil, balsamic vinegar and salt. Bake for 20 minutes. Add the garlic and bake for a further 15 minutes. Cool and squeeze or peel the garlic from its skin.
2 Grease a 34 x 10 cm (14 x 4 inch) loose-based fluted tart tin. Lay a sheet of pastry over each end of the tin, so that they overlap the edges and each other. Seal the sheets together with egg and trim the edges. Cover with baking paper and baking beads. Bake for 15 minutes. Remove the paper and beads and bake for 10 minutes.

3 Place the roasted tomatoes along the centre of the tart and fill the gaps with the garlic and halved bocconcini. Bake for a further 10 minutes and serve with basil leaves.

NUTRITION PER SERVE
Protein 25 g; Fat 40 g; Carbohydrate 30 g;
Dietary Fibre 3 g; Cholesterol 115 mg;
2580 kJ (615 cal)

Place the tomatoes on a baking tray and drizzle with oil, vinegar and salt.

Let the roasted garlic cloves cool, then squeeze or peel them from their skins.

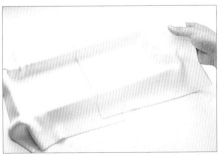
Place a sheet of pastry over each end of the tin, so they overlap in the middle.

CHEESE AND SPINACH PANCAKES

Preparation time: 40 minutes
Total cooking time: 50 minutes
Serves 4

250 g (8 oz) cooked, drained
    English spinach, chopped
1/2 cup (125 g/4 oz) ricotta cheese
1/4 cup (30 g/1 oz) grated Cheddar
freshly grated nutmeg
1/4 cup (25 g/3/4 oz) grated Parmesan
1/2 teaspoon paprika
1/2 cup (40 g/11/4 oz) fresh breadcrumbs

BATTER
1 cup (125 g/4 oz) plain flour
11/4 cups (315 ml/10 fl oz) milk
1 egg
butter, for cooking

CHEESE SAUCE
2 tablespoons butter
1/4 cup (30 g/1 oz) plain flour
13/4 cups (440 ml/14 fl oz) milk
1 cup (125 g/4 oz) grated Cheddar

1 Put the spinach, cheeses and nutmeg in a bowl and mix well.
2 To make the batter, sift the flour and a pinch of salt into a bowl. Add half the milk and the egg. Whisk until smooth; add the remaining milk. Heat a teaspoon of butter in a frying pan and pour in a thin layer of batter. Cook the base until golden, then flip. The batter should make 8 pancakes.
3 To make the cheese sauce, melt the butter over low heat, stir in the flour until smooth and cook for 1 minute. Remove from the heat and slowly stir in the milk. Bring to the boil, stirring constantly. Remove from the heat and add salt and pepper and the grated cheese.
4 Preheat the oven to moderate 180°C (350°F/ Gas 4). Divide the filling among the pancakes, roll up and put in a greased ovenproof dish. Pour cheese sauce over the pancakes. Mix the Parmesan, paprika and breadcrumbs together and sprinkle over the sauce. Bake for 30 minutes, or until golden brown.

NUTRITION PER SERVE
Protein 18 g; Fat 17 g; Carbohydrate 34 g;
Dietary Fibre 3 g; Cholesterol 96 mg;
1511 kJ (360 Cal)

Put the spinach, cheese, pepper and nutmeg in a bowl and mix well.

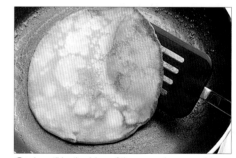

Cook until both sides of the pancake are golden, then remove with a spatula.

Remove the sauce from the heat and add salt and pepper, to taste, and grated cheese.

Divide the filling among the pancakes, roll up and put in the greased dish.

RATATOUILLE TARTE TATIN

Preparation time: 45 minutes +
  20 minutes refrigeration
Total cooking time: 50 minutes
Serves 6

1½ cups (185 g/6 oz) plain flour
90 g (3 oz) butter, chopped
1 egg
1 tablespoon oil
30 g (1 oz) butter, extra
2 zucchini, halved lengthways and
  sliced
250 g (8 oz) eggplant, diced
1 red capsicum, diced
1 green capsicum, diced
1 large red onion, diced
250 g (8 oz) cherry tomatoes, halved
2 tablespoons balsamic vinegar
½ cup (60 g/2 oz) grated Cheddar
300 g (10 oz) sour cream
3 tablespoons good-quality pesto

1 Sift the flour into a bowl and add the butter. Rub the butter into the flour with your fingertips until it resembles fine breadcrumbs. Make a well in the centre and add the egg (and 2 tablespoons water if the mixture is too dry). Mix with a flat-bladed knife, using a cutting action, until the mixture comes together in beads. Gather the dough together and lift onto a floured work surface. Press into a ball, flatten slightly into a disc, then wrap in plastic wrap and refrigerate for 20 minutes.

2 Preheat the oven to moderately hot 200°C (400°F/Gas 6). Grease a 25 cm (12 inch) springform tin and line with baking paper. Heat the oil and extra butter in a large frying pan and cook the zucchini, eggplant, capsicums and onion over high heat for 8 minutes, or until just soft. Add the tomatoes and vinegar and cook for 3–4 minutes.

3 Place the tin on a baking tray and neatly lay the vegetables in the tin, then sprinkle with cheese. Roll the dough out between two sheets of baking paper to a 28 cm (11 inch) circle. Remove the paper and invert the pastry into the tin over the filling. Use a spoon handle to tuck the edge of the pastry down the side of the tin. Bake for 30–35 minutes (some liquid will leak out), then leave to stand for 1–2 minutes. Remove from the tin and place on a serving plate, pastry-side-down. Mix the sour cream and pesto together in a small bowl. Serve with the tarte tatin.

NUTRITION PER SERVE
Protein 10 g; Fat 40 g; Carbohydrate 29 g;
Dietary Fibre 4.5 g; Cholesterol 144 mg;
2277 kJ (544 Cal)

Mix with a flat-bladed knife until the mixture comes together in beads.

Add the cherry tomatoes and balsamic vinegar and cook for 3–4 minutes.

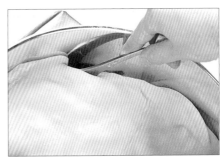
Use a spoon handle to tuck the edge of the pastry down the side of the tin.

CARAMELIZED ONION, ROCKET AND BLUE CHEESE TARTS

Preparation time: 30 minutes +
  30 minutes refrigeration
Total cooking time: 1 hour 10 minutes
Serves 6

PASTRY
2 cups (250 g/8 oz) plain flour
125 g (4 oz) butter, chilled and cut
  into cubes
¼ cup (25 g/¾ oz) finely grated
  Parmesan
1 egg, lightly beaten
¼ cup (60 ml/2 fl oz) chilled water

FILLING
2 tablespoons olive oil
3 onions, thinly sliced
100 g (3½ oz) baby rocket leaves
100 g (3½ oz) blue cheese, lightly
  crumbled
3 eggs, lightly beaten
¼ cup (60 ml/2 fl oz) cream
½ cup (50 g/1¾ oz) finely grated
  Parmesan
pinch grated fresh nutmeg

1 To make the pastry, sift the flour into a large bowl and add the butter. Rub the butter into the flour with your fingertips until it resembles fine breadcrumbs. Stir in the Parmesan.
2 Make a well in the centre of the dry ingredients, add the egg and water and mix with a flat-bladed knife, using a cutting action, until the mixture comes together in beads.
3 Gently gather the dough together and lift out onto a lightly floured work surface. Press into a ball and flatten it slightly into a disc, wrap in plastic wrap and refrigerate for 30 minutes.
4 Preheat the oven to moderately hot 200°C (400°F/Gas 6). Divide the pastry into six. Roll the dough out between two sheets of baking paper to fit six round 8 cm x 3 cm deep (3 inch x 1¼ inch deep) fluted loose-bottomed tart tins, remove the top sheet of paper and invert the pastry into the tins. Use a small ball of pastry to help press the pastry into the tins, allowing any excess to hang over the sides. Roll the rolling pin over the tins to cut off any excess.

5 Line the pastry shells with a piece of crumpled baking paper and pour in some baking beads or uncooked rice. Bake for 10 minutes, then remove the paper and beads and return the pastry to the oven for 10 minutes, or until the base is dry and golden. Cool slightly. Reduce the oven to moderate 180°C (350°F/Gas 4).
6 Heat the oil in a large frying pan, add the onion and cook over medium heat for 20 minutes, or until the onion is caramelized and golden. (Don't rush this step.)

7 Add the rocket and stir until wilted. Remove from the pan and cool.
8 Divide the onion mixture among the tart bases, then sprinkle with the blue cheese. Whisk together the eggs, cream, Parmesan and nutmeg and pour over each of the tarts. Place on a baking tray and bake for 25 minutes. Serve hot or cold with a green salad.

NUTRITION PER SERVE
Protein 18 g; Fat 40 g; Carbohydrate 33 g; Dietary Fibre 2.5 g; Cholesterol 215 mg; 2388 kJ (570 Cal)

Rub the butter into the flour until it resembles fine breadcrumbs.

Use a small ball of pastry to press the pastry into the tins.

MUSHROOM MOUSSAKA

Preparation time: 20 minutes
Total cooking time: 1 hour
Serves 4–6

1 eggplant (250 g/8 oz), cut into
   1 cm (1/2 inch) slices
1 large potato, cut into 1 cm (1/2 inch)
   slices
30 g (1 oz) butter
1 onion, finely chopped
2 cloves garlic, finely chopped
500 g (1 lb) flat mushrooms, sliced
400 g (13 oz) can chopped tomatoes
1/2 teaspoon sugar
40 g (11/4 oz) butter, extra
1/3 cup (40 g/11/4 oz) plain flour
2 cups (500 ml/16 fl oz) milk
1 egg, lightly beaten
40 g (11/4 oz) grated Parmesan

1 Preheat the oven to hot 220°C
(425°F/Gas 7). Line a large baking
tray with foil and brush with oil. Put
the eggplant and potato in a single
layer on the tray and sprinkle with
salt and pepper. Bake for 20 minutes.
2 Melt the butter in a large frying pan
over medium heat. Add the onion and
cook, stirring, for 3–4 minutes, or until
soft. Add the garlic and cook for
1 minute, or until fragrant. Increase the
heat to high, add the mushrooms and
stir continuously for 2–3 minutes, or
until soft. Add the tomato, reduce the
heat and simmer rapidly for 8 minutes,
or until reduced. Stir in the sugar.
3 Melt the extra butter in a large
saucepan over low heat. Add the flour
and cook for 1 minute, or until pale
and foaming. Remove from the heat
and gradually stir in the milk. Return
to the heat and stir constantly until it
boils and thickens. Reduce the heat

and simmer for 2 minutes. Remove
from the heat and, when the bubbles
subside, stir in the egg and Parmesan.
4 Reduce the oven to moderate 180°C
(350°F/Gas 4). Grease a shallow
1.5 litre ovenproof dish. Spoon one
third of the mushroom mixture into
the dish. Cover with potato and top
with half the remaining mushrooms,
then the eggplant. Finish with the

remaining mushrooms, pour on
the sauce and smooth the top. Bake
for 30–35 minutes, or until the edges
bubble. Leave to rest for 10 minutes
before serving.

NUTRITION PER SERVE (6)
Protein 12 g; Fat 16 g; Carbohydrate 18 g;
Dietary Fibre 5 g; Cholesterol 77 mg;
1125 kJ (268 Cal)

A small amount of sugar added to the tomato
mixture will bring out the flavours.

Remove the saucepan from the heat and stir in
the egg and Parmesan.

Cover the tomato and mushroom mixture with the
potato slices.

PUMPKIN AND FETA PIE

Preparation time: 30 minutes +
  cooling + 20 minutes refrigeration
Total cooking time: 1 hour 25 minutes
Serves 6

700 g (1 lb 7 oz) butternut pumpkin,
  cubed
4 cloves garlic, unpeeled
5 tablespoons olive oil
2 small red onions, halved and sliced
1 tablespoon balsamic vinegar
1 tablespoon soft brown sugar
100 g (3¹/2 oz) feta, broken into
  small pieces
1 tablespoon chopped fresh rosemary

PASTRY
2 cups (250 g/8 oz) plain flour
125 g (4 oz) butter, chilled and cubed
¹/2 cup (60 g/2 oz) grated Parmesan
3–4 tablespoons iced water

1 Preheat the oven to 200°C (400°F/
Gas 6). Place the pumpkin and garlic
cloves on a baking tray, drizzle with
2 tablespoons oil and bake for
25–30 minutes, or until the pumpkin is
tender. Transfer the pumpkin to a large
bowl and the garlic to a plate. Leave
the pumpkin to cool.
2 Meanwhile, heat 2 tablespoons oil
in a pan, add the onion and cook over
medium heat, stirring occasionally, for
10 minutes. Add the vinegar and sugar
and cook for 15 minutes, or until the
onion is caramelised. Remove from the
heat and add to the pumpkin. Leave to
cool completely.
3 While the vegetables are cooling,
make the pastry. Sift the flour and
1 teaspoon salt into a large bowl and
rub in the butter with your fingertips
until the mixture resembles fine
breadcrumbs. Stir in the Parmesan.
Make a well, add almost all the water
and mix with a flat-bladed knife, using
a cutting action, until the mixture
comes together in beads. Add a little
more water if necessary to bring the
dough together.
4 Gather the dough together and lift
onto a lightly floured work surface.
Press together into a ball and flatten
slightly into a disc. Cover in plastic
wrap and refrigerate for 20 minutes.
5 Add the feta and rosemary to the
pumpkin. Squeeze out the garlic flesh
and mix it through the vegetables.
Season, to taste.
6 Roll out the dough between two
sheets of baking paper to a 35 cm
(14 inch) circle. Remove the top sheet
of paper and place the bottom paper
with the pastry on a tray. Arrange the
pumpkin and feta mixture on top,
leaving a 6 cm (2¹/2 inch) border. Fold
over the edges, pleating as you fold,
and bake for 30 minutes, or until crisp
and golden.

NUTRITION PER SERVE
Protein 14 g; Fat 39 g; Carbohydrate 42 g;
Dietary Fibre 4 g; Cholesterol 73 mg;
2360 kJ (565 cal)

Fold the edges of the pastry over the pumpkin
and feta filling.

SPICY BEANS ON BAKED SWEET POTATO

Preparation time: 20 minutes
Total cooking time: 1 hour 30 minutes
Serves 6

3 orange sweet potatoes
    (500 g/1 lb each)
1 tablespoon olive oil
1 large onion, chopped
3 cloves garlic, crushed
2 teaspoons ground cumin
1 teaspoon ground coriander
1/2 teaspoon chilli powder
400 g (13 oz) can chopped tomatoes
1 cup (250 ml/8 fl oz) vegetable
    stock
1 large zucchini, cubed
1 green capsicum, cubed
310 g (10 oz) can corn kernels,
    drained
2 x 400 g (13 oz) cans red kidney
    beans, rinsed and drained
3 tablespoons chopped fresh
    coriander leaves
light sour cream and grated reduced-
    fat Cheddar, to serve

1 Preheat the oven to hot 210°C (415°F/Gas 6–7). Rinse the sweet potatoes, then pierce with a small sharp knife. Place them on a baking tray and bake for 1–1½ hours, or until soft when tested with a skewer or sharp knife.
2 Meanwhile, heat the oil in a large saucepan and cook the onion over medium heat for about 5 minutes, stirring occasionally, until very soft and golden. Add the garlic and spices, and cook, stirring, for 1 minute.
3 Add the tomato and stock, stir well, then add the vegetables and beans. Bring to the boil, then reduce the heat and simmer, partially covered, for 20 minutes. Uncover, increase the heat slightly, and cook for a further 10–15 minutes, or until the liquid has reduced and thickened. Stir in the coriander leaves just before serving.
4 To serve, cut the sweet potatoes in half lengthways. Spoon the vegetable mixture over the top. Add a dollop of light sour cream and sprinkle with grated Cheddar cheese.

NUTRITION PER SERVE
Protein 15 g; Fat 5 g; Carbohydrate 72 g;
Dietary Fibre 17 g; Cholesterol 0 mg;
1665 kJ (397 Cal)

Cook the spicy vegetable mixture until the liquid has reduced.

Cut the baked sweet potatoes in half lengthways and top with the spicy beans.

TOMATO AND THYME QUICHE

Preparation time: 35 minutes +
  30 minutes refrigeration
Total cooking time: 45 minutes
Serves 8

1½ cups (185 g/6 oz) plain flour
125 g (4 oz) butter, chilled and cubed
1 egg yolk
2–3 tablespoons iced water

FILLING
425 g (14 oz) can tomatoes
4 eggs
300 g (10 oz) sour cream
¼ cup (25 g/¾ oz) grated Parmesan
2 spring onions, finely chopped
1–2 tablespoons chopped fresh
  thyme

1 Preheat the oven to 210°C (415°F/Gas 6–7). Sift the flour into a bowl and rub in the butter until the mixture resembles fine breadcrumbs. Add the combined egg yolk and water and mix to a soft dough. Turn out onto a lightly floured surface and gather into a ball.

Wrap in plastic and refrigerate for 30 minutes.
2 Roll out the pastry to line a shallow 23 cm (9 inch) tart tin, trimming off the excess. Cover with baking paper and spread with a layer of baking beads or rice. Bake for 10 minutes, then discard the paper and beads and cook for a further 5 minutes or until golden.
3 Drain the tomatoes and halve lengthways. Place, cut-side-down, on paper towels to drain. Beat together the eggs and sour cream and stir in the cheese and spring onion.
4 Pour the filling into the pastry shell. Arrange the tomatoes, cut-side-down, over the filling. Sprinkle with thyme and pepper. Reduce the oven to 180°C (350°F/Gas 4) and bake for 30 minutes or until the filling is set and golden.

NUTRITION PER SERVE
Protein 9 g; Fat 25 g; Carbohydrate 20 g;
Dietary Fibre 2 g; Cholesterol 105 mg;
1345 kJ (320 cal)

STORAGE: The pastry shell can be blind baked a day in advance and stored in an airtight container.

Drain the canned tomatoes and cut them in half lengthways. Put on paper towel to drain further.

Blind bake the pastry shell until it is dry and golden before pouring in the filling.

CHEESE AND ONION PIE

Preparation time: 25 minutes +
   10 minutes cooling
Total cooking time: 45 minutes
Serves 4

2 tablespoons olive oil
2 onions, chopped
1¹/₂ cups (185 g/6 oz) grated Cheddar
1 tablespoon chopped fresh flat-leaf
   parsley
1 teaspoon English mustard
2 teaspoons Worcestershire sauce
2 eggs, beaten
2 sheets puff pastry

1 Preheat the oven to 190°C (375°F/ Gas 5). Heat the oil in a large frying pan over medium heat, add the onion and cook for 5–7 minutes, or until soft and golden. Transfer to a bowl and allow to cool for 10 minutes.
2 Add the cheese, parsley, mustard and Worcestershire sauce to the onion and mix well. Add half the egg to the bowl and season well.
3 Cut each sheet of pastry into a 23 cm (9 inch) circle. Lay one sheet of pastry on a lined baking tray. Spread the filling over the pastry base, piling it higher in the middle and leaving a narrow border. Lightly brush the border with some of the beaten egg and place the second sheet on top, stretching it slightly to neatly fit the bottom. Press and seal the edges well and brush the top with the remaining beaten egg. Cut two slits in the top for steam to escape.
4 Bake for 10 minutes, then reduce the heat to 180°C (350°F/ Gas 4) and cook for another 20–25 minutes, or until the pastry is crisp and golden.

NUTRITION PER SERVE
Protein 21 g; Fat 47 g; Carbohydrate 34 g; Dietary Fibre 2 g; Cholesterol 158 mg; 2625 kJ (630 cal)

Mix the cheese, parsley, mustard and Worcestershire sauce through the onion.

Brush the border of the pastry with some of the beaten egg.

Lift the second pastry circle over the cheese and onion filling.

FRESH HERB TART

Preparation time: 40 minutes +
  30 minutes refrigeration
Total cooking time: 1 hour 10 minutes
Serves 4–6

1¼ cups (150 g/5 oz) plain flour
100 g (3½ oz) butter, chilled and
  cubed
1–2 tablespoons iced water

250 g (8 oz) light sour cream
½ cup (125 ml/4 fl oz) thick cream
2 eggs, lightly beaten
1 tablespoon chopped fresh thyme
2 tablespoons chopped fresh parsley
1 tablespoon chopped fresh oregano

1 Put the flour and butter in a food processor and process for 15 seconds, or until the mixture resembles fine breadcrumbs. Add the water and process in short bursts until the mixture just comes together, adding a little more water if needed. Turn out onto a floured surface and gather into a ball. Cover with plastic wrap and refrigerate for at least 20 minutes. Roll out on a sheet of baking paper to line a 34 x 10 cm (14 x 4 inch) loose-based tart tin. Trim off the excess pastry. Refrigerate for 10 minutes. Preheat the oven to 200°C (400°F/Gas 6).
2 Cover the pastry shell with baking paper and fill evenly with baking beads or rice. Place on a baking tray and bake for 20 minutes. Remove the

paper and beads and reduce the oven to 180°C (350°F/Gas 4). Cook for 15–20 minutes, or until golden and dry. Cool.
3 Whisk together the sour cream, thick cream and eggs until smooth. Then stir in the herbs and season.
4 Place the pastry shell on a baking tray and pour in the filling. Bake for 25–30 minutes, or until set. Allow to stand for 15 minutes before serving.

NUTRITION PER SERVE (6)
Protein 6 g; Fat 25 g; Carbohydrate 20 g;
Dietary Fibre 1 g; Cholesterol 130 mg;
1340 kJ (320 cal)

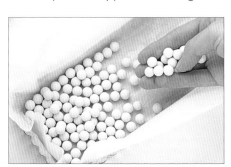

If you don't have baking beads for blind baking, use dry rice or beans.

Put the sour cream, thick cream and eggs in a bowl and whisk together.

Put the pastry shell on a baking tray before cooking to catch any drips.

ASPARAGUS AND ARTICHOKE QUICHES

Preparation time: 40 minutes +
  30 minutes refrigeration
Total cooking time: 40 minutes
Makes 6

1¼ cups (150 g/5 oz) plain flour
90 g (3 oz) butter, chilled and cubed
½ cup (60 g/2 oz) grated Cheddar
2–3 tablespoons iced water

FILLING
1 bunch (155 g/5 oz) asparagus,
  trimmed, cut into bite-size pieces
2 eggs
⅓ cup (80 ml/2¾ fl oz) cream
⅓ cup (40 g/1¼ oz) grated Gruyère
  cheese
150 g (5 oz) marinated artichoke
  hearts, quartered

1 Process the flour and butter for about 15 seconds until crumbly. Add the cheese and water. Process in short bursts until the mixture comes together. Add a little more water if needed. Turn out onto a floured surface and gather into a ball. Wrap in plastic and refrigerate for 30 minutes.
2 Preheat the oven to 190°C (375°F/ Gas 5). Grease six 8.5 cm (3¼ inch) loose-based fluted tart tins. Roll out the pastry to fit the tins, trimming off the excess. Prick the pastry bases with a fork, place on a baking tray and bake for 10–12 minutes, or until the pastry is light and golden.
3 To make the filling, blanch the asparagus pieces in boiling salted water. Drain and refresh in iced water. Lightly beat the eggs, cream and half the cheese together and season with salt and black pepper.

4 Divide the artichokes and asparagus among the pastry shells, pour the egg and cream mixture over the top and sprinkle with the remaining cheese. Bake for 25 minutes, or until the filling is set and golden. If the pastry is overbrowning, cover with foil.

NUTRITION PER QUICHE
Protein 10 g; Fat 30 g; Carbohydrate 20 g;
Dietary Fibre 2 g; Cholesterol 150 mg;
1665 kJ (395 cal)

Cut the marinated artichoke hearts into quarters.

Process in short bursts until the mixture just comes together.

Divide the artichoke and asparagus evenly among the pastry shells.

MUSHROOM QUICHE WITH PARSLEY PASTRY

Preparation time: 30 minutes +
    50 minutes refrigeration
Total cooking time: 1 hour
Serves 4–6

1¼ cups (155 g/5 oz) plain flour
¼ cup (15 g/½ oz) chopped fresh
    parsley
90 g (3 oz) butter, chilled and cubed
1 egg yolk
2 tablespoons iced water

FILLING
30 g (1 oz) butter
1 red onion, chopped
175 g (6 oz) button mushrooms, sliced
1 teaspoon lemon juice
⅓ cup (20 g/¾ oz) chopped fresh
    parsley
⅓ cup (20 g/¾ oz) chopped chives
1 egg, lightly beaten
⅓ cup (80 ml/2¾ oz) cream

1 Process the flour, parsley and butter for 15 seconds, or until crumbly. Add the egg yolk and water. Process in short bursts until the mixture comes together. Add a little more water if needed. Turn out onto a floured surface and gather into a ball. Cover with plastic wrap and refrigerate for at least 30 minutes.

2 Roll out the pastry between two sheets of baking paper until large enough to fit a 35 x 10 cm (14 x 4 inch) loose-based tart tin. Trim away the excess pastry. Refrigerate for 20 minutes. Preheat the oven to 190°C (375°F/Gas 5). Cover the pastry with baking paper and spread with a layer of baking beads or rice. Bake for 15 minutes. Remove the paper and

beads and bake for 10 minutes, or until the pastry is dry. Reduce the oven to 180°C (350°F/Gas 4).

3 To make the mushroom filling, melt the butter in a pan and cook the onion for 2–3 minutes until soft. Add the mushrooms and cook, stirring, for 2–3 minutes until soft. Stir in the lemon juice and herbs. Mix the egg and cream together and season.

4 Spread the mushroom filling into the pastry shell and pour over the egg and cream. Bake for 25–30 minutes, or until the filling has set.

NUTRITION PER SERVE (6)
Protein 6 g; Fat 25 g; Carbohydrate 20 g;
Dietary Fibre 2 g; Cholesterol 130 mg;
1350 kJ (320 cal)

Place the flour and parsley in a food processor and add the butter.

The easiest way to line the tin with pastry is to roll the pastry over the rolling pin to lift it.

Pour the combined egg and cream over the mushroom filling.

BAKED POLENTA WITH THREE CHEESES

Preparation time: 20 minutes
+ 2 hours chilling
Total cooking time: 45 minutes
Serves 4

POLENTA
2¹/₂ cups (600 ml/20 fl oz) vegetable
stock
2 cups (300 g/10 oz) polenta (see
NOTE)
¹/₂ cup (60 g/2 oz) grated Parmesan

CHEESE FILLING
100 g (3¹/₂ oz) havarti cheese, sliced
100 g (3¹/₂ oz) mascarpone cheese
100 g (3¹/₂ oz) blue cheese, crumbled
100 g (3¹/₂ oz) butter, sliced thinly
¹/₂ cup (60 g/2 oz) grated Parmesan

1 To make the polenta, brush a 7-cup
(1.75 litre/56 fl oz) loaf tin with oil. Put
the stock and 2 cups (500 ml/16 fl oz)
water in a large pan and bring to the
boil. Add the polenta and stir for
10 minutes until very thick.
2 Remove from the heat and stir in the
Parmesan. Spread into the tin and
smooth the surface. Refrigerate for
2 hours, then cut into about 30 thin
slices. Preheat the oven to moderate
180°C (350°F/Gas 4).
3 Brush a large ovenproof dish with
oil. Place a layer of polenta slices on
the base. Top with a layer of half the
combined havarti, mascarpone and
blue cheeses and half the butter. Add
another layer of polenta and top with
the remainder of the three cheeses and
butter. Add a final layer of polenta and
sprinkle the Parmesan on top. Bake for
30 minutes, or until a golden crust
forms. Serve immediately.

NUTRITION PER SERVE
Protein 20 g; Fat 38 g; Carbohydrate 35 g;
Dietary Fibre 1.5 g; Cholesterol 113 mg;
2351 kJ (560 cal)

NOTE: Polenta is also known as
cornmeal and is available from most
supermarkets and delicatessens.
Havarti is a Danish cheese with a
full flavour.

Add the polenta to the stock and water and stir
constantly until very thick.

Use the back of a spoon to spread the polenta in
the tin.

Build up the layers of sliced polenta, butter and
different cheeses.

Add the final layer of sliced polenta and then
sprinkle with Parmesan cheese.

ORZO AND GREEK CHEESE BAKE

Preparation time: 15 minutes
Total cooking time: 40 minutes
Serves 6

2 cups (415 g/13 oz) orzo
60 g (2 oz) butter
6 spring onions, chopped
450 g (14 oz) English spinach, trimmed and chopped
2 tablespoons plain flour
1.25 litres milk
250 g (8 oz) kefalotyri cheese, grated (see NOTE)
250 g (8 oz) marinated feta, drained
3 tablespoons chopped fresh dill

1 Preheat the oven to moderately hot 190°C (375°F/Gas 5). Cook the pasta in a large pan of rapidly boiling salted water until *al dente*. Drain well and return to the pan keep warm. Heat 1 tablespoon of the butter in a large saucepan over high heat and cook the spring onion for 30 seconds. Add the spinach and stir for 1 minute, or until wilted. Season and stir into the pasta.
2 Put the remaining butter in the saucepan in which the spinach was cooked. Melt over low heat, then stir in the flour and cook for 1 minute, or until pale and foaming. Remove from the heat and gradually stir in the milk. Return to the heat and stir constantly for 5 minutes, or until the sauce boils and thickens. Add two-thirds of the kefalotyri and all of the feta and stir for 2 minutes until melted. Remove from the heat and stir in the dill.
3 Combine the pasta mixture with the cheese sauce, season to taste and pour into a lightly greased 2.5-litre oven-proof dish. Sprinkle the remaining cheese on top and bake for 15 minutes, or until golden.

NUTRITION PER SERVE
Protein 31 g; Fat 34 g; Carbohydrate 63 g; Dietary Fibre 6 g; Cholesterol 103 mg; 2835 kJ (680 cal)

NOTE: Kefalotyri is a hard Greek sheep's milk cheese; it is similar to Parmesan.

Cook the spinach until wilted, then season well and stir into the orzo.

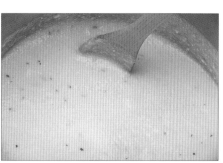

Cook the sauce, stirring constantly, until it boils and thickens.

Mix together the pasta and spinach with the cheese sauce.

POTATO AND ZUCCHINI TART

Preparation time: 25 minutes +
  15 minutes refrigeration
Total cooking time: 1 hour 20 minutes
Serves 6

1 1/2 cups (185 g/6 oz) plain flour
125 g (4 oz) butter, chilled and cubed
1 egg yolk
1–2 tablespoons iced water

FILLING
450 g (14 oz) floury potatoes, peeled
  and roughly chopped
1/3 cup (40 g/1 1/4 oz) plain flour
125 g (4 oz) Jarlsberg cheese, grated
1/3 cup (80 ml/2 3/4 fl oz) cream
2 eggs, separated
2–3 small zucchini, thinly sliced
  lengthways
4 sprigs fresh thyme, to garnish

1 Grease a 25 cm (10 inch) loose-based flan tin.

2 To make the pastry, put the flour in a bowl with 1/2 teaspoon of salt. Rub in the butter with your fingertips, until the mixture resembles fine crumbs. Add the egg yolk and water and mix with a knife to form a rough dough. Turn out onto a lightly floured surface and work into a smooth ball, then wrap in plastic and refrigerate for 15 minutes. Preheat the oven to 190°C (375°F/Gas 5).

3 On a lightly floured surface, roll out the dough large enough to fit the tin. Trim off the excess pastry. Cover with baking paper and fill with baking beads or rice. Bake for 10 minutes and discard the paper and beads. Bake for another 5–10 minutes.

4 To make the filling, boil or steam the potato until tender. Drain, cool for 5 minutes and mash. Mix in the flour and cheese, stir in 2/3 cup (170 ml/5 1/2 fl oz) of water and, when loosely incorporated, add the cream. Whisk until smooth, add the egg yolks and combine well. Season with salt and white pepper. Beat the egg whites in a small bowl until stiff peaks form, fold into the potato mixture and gently pour into the pie crust.

5 Arrange the zucchini over the pie in a decorative pattern. Decorate with thyme and bake for 35–45 minutes, until set and golden brown. Serve hot or at room temperature.

NUTRITION PER SERVE
Protein 15 g; Fat 30 g; Carbohydrate 40 g;
Dietary Fibre 3 g; Cholesterol 185 mg;
2105 kJ (500 cal)

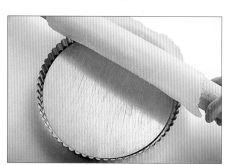

The easiest way to line the tin with pastry is to lift the pastry over the rolling pin.

Blind bake the pastry base before filling it with the potato mixture.

Arrange the thin slices of zucchini over the pie in a decorative pattern.

VEGETABLE PIE WITH CHEESE TOPPING

Preparation time: 25 minutes +
   20 minutes refrigeration
Total cooking time: 1 hour 30 minutes
Serves 6

1 cup (125 g/4 oz) plain flour
60 g (2 oz) butter, chilled and cubed
1 egg yolk
2 teaspoons poppy seeds
1–2 tablespoons iced water

FILLING
30 g (1 oz) butter
2 tablespoons oil
1 onion, cut into thin wedges
1 leek, sliced
3 potatoes, cut into large chunks
300 g (10 oz) orange sweet potato,
   cut into large chunks
300 g (10 oz) pumpkin, cubed
200 g (6¹/₂ oz) swede, peeled and
   cubed
1 cup (250 ml/8 fl oz) vegetable stock
1 red capsicum, cubed
200 g (6¹/₂ oz) broccoli, cut into large
   florets
2 zucchini, cut into large pieces
1 cup (125 g/4 oz) grated Cheddar

1 Preheat the oven to 200°C (400°F/ Gas 6). To make the pastry, sift the flour into a large bowl and add the butter. Rub in the butter with your fingertips until it resembles fine breadcrumbs. Make a well in the centre and add the egg yolk, poppy seeds and water and mix with a flat-bladed knife, using a cutting action, until the mixture comes together in beads. Gently gather together and lift out onto a lightly floured work surface. Press into a disc, wrap in plastic and refrigerate for 20 minutes.
2 Roll out the dough between two sheets of baking paper, then fit into a 23 cm (9 inch) pie plate. Trim away any excess pastry. Prick the base with a fork and bake for 15–20 minutes, or until dry and golden.
3 Heat the butter and oil in a large saucepan and cook the onion and leek over medium heat for 5 minutes, or until soft and golden. Add the potato, sweet potato, pumpkin and swede and cook, stirring occasionally, until the vegetables start to soften. Add the stock and simmer for 30 minutes.
4 Add the remaining vegetables, reduce the heat and simmer for 20 minutes, or until the vegetables are soft—some may break up slightly. The mixture should be just mushy. Season and leave to cool a little.
5 Spoon the filling into the shell, sprinkle with cheese and cook under a medium grill for 5–10 minutes, or until the cheese is golden brown.

NUTRITION PER SERVE
Protein 14 g; Fat 27 g; Carbohydrate 32 g; Dietary Fibre 6.5 g; Cholesterol 90 mg; 1790 kJ (428 cal)

Prick the base of the pastry all over with a fork and bake until dry and golden.

Cook the vegetables until they are very soft when tested with a knife.

FILO VEGETABLE STRUDEL

Preparation time: 30 minutes +
    30 minutes standing
Total cooking time: 1 hour
Serves 6–8

1 large eggplant, sliced
1 red capsicum
3 zucchini, sliced lengthways
2 tablespoons olive oil
6 sheets filo pastry
50 g (1³/₄ oz) baby English spinach
    leaves
60 g (2 oz) feta cheese, sliced

1 Preheat the oven to 190°C (375°F/ Gas 5). Sprinkle the eggplant slices with a little salt and leave to drain in a colander for 30 minutes. Pat dry with paper towels.
2 Cut the capsicum into quarters and place, skin-side-up, under a hot grill for 10 minutes, or until the skin blackens. Peel away the skin. Brush the eggplant and zucchini with olive oil and grill for 5–10 minutes, or until golden brown. Set aside to cool.
3 Brush one sheet of filo pastry at a time with olive oil, then lay them on top of each other. Place half the eggplant slices lengthways down the centre of the filo and top with a layer

of zucchini, capsicum, spinach and feta cheese. Repeat the layers until the vegetables and cheese are used up. Tuck in the ends of the pastry, then roll up like a parcel; brush lightly with oil and place on a baking tray. Bake for 35 minutes, or until golden brown.

NUTRITION PER SERVE (8)
Protein 4 g; Fat 7 g; Carbohydrate 9 g;
Dietary Fibre 3 g; Cholesterol 5 mg;
485 kJ (115 cal)

NOTE: Unopened packets of filo can be stored in the fridge for up to a month. Once opened, use within 2–3 days.

Cut a large eggplant into thin slices with a sharp knife, then sprinkle with salt.

Build up layers of eggplant, zucchini, capsicum, spinach and feta cheese.

Tuck in the ends of the pastry, then roll up like a parcel to make a strudel.

PUMPKIN TARTS

Preparation time: 20 minutes +
   30 minutes refrigeration
Total cooking time: 30 minutes
Serves 6

2 cups (250 g) plain flour
125 g (4 oz) butter, chilled and cubed
1/2 cup (125 ml/4 fl oz) iced water

FILLING
1.2 kg (2 lb 7 oz) pumpkin, cut into
   chunks
1/2 cup (125 g/4 oz) sour cream or
   cream cheese
sweet chilli sauce, to serve

1 Sift the flour and a pinch of salt into a large bowl and add the butter. Rub into the flour with your fingertips until it resembles fine breadcrumbs. Make a well in the centre, add the water and mix with a flat-bladed knife, using a cutting action, until the mixture comes together in beads. Gently gather the dough together and lift out onto a lightly floured work surface. Press together into a ball, wrap in plastic and refrigerate for 30 minutes.
2 Preheat the oven to 200°C (400°F/ Gas 6). Divide the pastry into six balls and roll each one out to fit a 10 cm (4 inch) pie dish. Trim the edges and prick the bases all over. Place on a baking tray and bake for 15 minutes, or until lightly golden, pressing down any pastry that puffs up. Cool, then remove from the tins.
3 To make the filling, steam the pumpkin pieces for about 15 minutes, or until tender.
4 Place a tablespoon of sour cream in the middle of each tart and pile the pumpkin pieces on top. Season and drizzle with sweet chilli sauce to taste. Return to the oven for a couple of minutes to heat through.

NUTRITION PER SERVE
Protein 9 g; Fat 26 g; Carbohydrate 44 g; Dietary Fibre 4 g; Cholesterol 80 mg; 1876 kJ (448 cal)

VARIATION: Instead of steaming, roast the pumpkin with garlic, olive oil and fresh thyme.

Fit the pastry into the pie dishes, trim to fit, then prick the bases.

Pile the steamed pumpkin pieces on top of the sour cream.

FETA, BASIL AND OLIVE QUICHE

Preparation time: 40 minutes +
  25 minutes refrigeration
Total cooking time: 40 minutes
Serves 6

1¼ cups (150 g/5 oz) self-raising
  flour, sifted
90 g (3 oz) butter, melted and cooled
¼ cup (60 ml/2 fl oz) milk

FILLING
250 g (8 oz) feta cheese, cubed
¼ cup (15 g/½ oz) fresh basil leaves,
  shredded
¼ cup (30 g/1 oz) sliced black olives
3 eggs, lightly beaten
⅓ cup (80 ml/2¾ fl oz) milk
⅓ cup (90 g/3 oz) sour cream

1 Grease a 23 cm (9 inch) loose-based tart tin. Place the flour in a large bowl and make a well in the centre. Add the butter and milk and stir until the mixture comes together to form a dough. Turn out onto a floured surface and gather into a ball. Refrigerate for 5 minutes. Roll out the pastry and place in the tin, pressing it well into the sides. Trim off any excess pastry. Refrigerate for 20 minutes. Preheat the oven to 200°C (400°F/Gas 6).
2 To make the filling, spread the feta evenly over the base of the pastry and top with the shredded basil and olives.
3 Whisk the eggs, milk and sour cream until smooth, then pour into the pastry shell. Bake for 15 minutes, reduce the oven to 180°C (350°F/Gas 4) and cook for a further 25 minutes, or until the filling is firmly set. Serve at room temperature.

NUTRITION PER SERVE
Protein 15 g; Fat 35 g; Carbohydrate 20 g;
Dietary Fibre 2 g; Cholesterol 180 mg;
1750 kJ (415 cal)

Cut the feta into cubes and shred the fresh basil leaves.

Add the melted butter and milk to the well in the centre of the flour.

Sprinkle the shredded basil and sliced olives over the quiche.

OVEN-BAKED POTATO, LEEK AND OLIVES

Preparation time: 20 minutes
Total cooking time: 1 hour
Serves 4–6

2 tablespoons extra virgin olive oil
1 leek, finely sliced
1½ cups (375 ml/12 fl oz) vegetable
  stock
2 teaspoons chopped fresh thyme
1 kg (2 lb) potatoes, unpeeled, cut into
  thin slices
6–8 pitted black olives, sliced
½ cup (60 g/2 oz) grated Parmesan
30 g (1 oz) butter, chopped

1 Preheat the oven to moderate 180°C (350°F/Gas 4). Brush a shallow 1.25 litre (40 fl oz) ovenproof dish with a little olive oil. Heat the remaining oil in a large pan and cook the leek over moderate heat until soft. Add the stock, thyme and potato. Cover and leave to simmer for 5 minutes.
2 Using tongs, lift out half the potato and put in the ovenproof dish. Sprinkle with olives and Parmesan and season with salt and pepper.
3 Layer with the remaining potato, then spoon the leek and stock mixture in at the side of the dish, keeping the top dry.
4 Scatter chopped butter over the potato and then bake, uncovered, for 50 minutes, or until cooked and golden brown. Leave in a warm place for about 10 minutes before serving.

NUTRITION PER SERVE (6)
Protein 7.5 g; Fat 13 g; Carbohydrate 23 g;
Dietary Fibre 3 g; Cholesterol 20 mg;
1019 kJ (243 Cal)

NOTE: Keeping the top layer of potato dry as you pour in the stock mixture will give the dish a crisp finish.

Cook the leek until soft, then add the stock, thyme and potato.

Lift out half the potato with tongs and put into an ovenproof dish.

Spoon the leek and stock mixture around the side, trying to keep the top dry.

Bake, uncovered, until the potatoes on top are golden brown.

CARROT AND LEEK SOY TART

Preparation time: 35 minutes +
  40 minutes chilling
Total cooking time: 1 hour 35 minutes
Serves 6–8

200 g (6½ oz) russet potatoes,
  quartered
1 tablespoon soy milk
1 cup (150 g/5 oz) wholemeal flour
½ cup (50 g/1¾ oz) soy flour
150 g (5 oz) soy spread or margarine
450 g (14 oz) carrots, diced
2 leeks (450 g/14 oz), thinly sliced
1 cup (250 ml/8 fl oz) vegetable stock
½ teaspoon sugar
1 tablespoon tomato paste
3 eggs
200 g (6½ oz) plain soy yoghurt
1 small carrot, extra
1 small leek, extra
1 tablespoon soy spread or
  margarine, extra

1 Boil the potato in salted water for 8–10 minutes, or until tender. Drain well, return to the pan, add the soy milk and season. Mash until smooth, then cool.

2 Place the flours in a bowl and rub in 100 g (3½ oz) of the soy spread until the mixture resembles fine bread-crumbs. Add the potato and bring together to form a ball. Cool, then wrap in plastic. Refrigerate for at least 30 minutes.

3 Preheat the oven to 200°C (400°F/ Gas 6). Roll out the dough to line a 23 cm (9 inch) loose-based tart tin and trim off the excess pastry. Chill for 10 minutes. Lin
baking paper

Remove the baking paper and beads and bake for 5 minutes, or until slightly golden. Reduce the oven to 180°C (350°F/Gas 4).

4 Melt the remaining soy spread in a saucepan. Add the carrot, leek and 2 tablespoons water and cook gently for 10 minutes, or until the liquid has evaporated. Add the stock and sugar and cook for 20 minutes, or until the vegetables are tender and all the liquid has been absorbed. Cool slightly, then add the tomato paste, eggs and yoghurt. Mix in a food processor until smooth. Season. Pour into the pastry

case and bake for 20–25 minutes, or until set and lightly golden on top.

5 Peel the extra carrot into thin ribbons with a vegetable peeler. Slice the extra leek lengthways into thin ribbons. Melt the extra soy spread in a frying pan and cook the carrot and leek for 8 minutes, or until soft. Pile in the centre of the tart and serve.

NUTRITION PER SERVE (8)
Protein 6 g; Fat 24 g; Carbohydrate 17 g;
Dietary Fibre 4.5 g; Cholesterol 68 mg;
1266 kJ (302 cal)

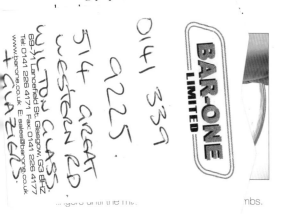

...gers until the m...   ...nbs.

Bring the dough together to form a ball, then wrap and refrigerate.

Cook the carrot, leek, stock and sugar until all the liquid has been absorbed.

SWEET POTATO AND FENNEL PIE

Preparation time: 20 minutes
+ 30 minutes refrigeration
+ 10 minutes draining
Total cooking time: 1 hour 10 minutes
Serves 6

2 fennel bulbs (500 g/1 lb), thick outer
   leaves removed, sliced
300 g (10 oz) sweet potato, cut into
   1 cm (1/2 inch) cubes
1 tablespoon dried juniper berries,
   ground
1/4 cup (60 ml/2 fl oz) olive oil
300 g (10 oz) ricotta
1 cup (100 g/3 1/2 oz) grated Parmesan
100 g (3 1/2 oz) ground almonds

6 sheets ready-rolled shortcrust pastry
milk, to glaze
3 sheets ready-rolled puff pastry

1 Preheat the oven to moderate 180°C
(350°F/Gas 4). Grease six 11 cm
(4 1/2 inch) (top) 9.5 cm (4 inch (base)
and 2.5 cm (1 inch) (deep) pie tins.
Place the fennel, sweet potato and
juniper berries in a deep roasting tin
and toss with the oil. Season, cover
with foil and cook for 35 minutes,
or until the vegetables have softened.
Drain any oil away, transfer to a bowl
and chill for 30 minutes, or until cold.
2 Combine the ricotta, Parmesan
and ground almonds in a large bowl.
Transfer to a sieve and sit over a bowl
for 10 minutes to drain away any
liquid from the ricotta.

3 Cut a 15 cm (6 inch) round from
each sheet of shortcrust pastry and
line the pie tins, leaving the excess
overhanging. Brush the rims with milk.
4 Divide the vegetables among the
pastry shells, then top with ricotta
mixture. Cut six 12 cm (4 3/4 inch)
rounds from the puff pastry, place
over the filled shells and trim. Seal
the edges with a fork and prick a
few holes in the tops. Brush with
milk, then bake for 35 minutes, or
until golden.

NUTRITION PER SERVE
Protein 29.5 g; Fat 86.5 g; Carbohydrate
104.5 g; Dietary Fibre 8.5 g; Cholesterol
102 mg; 5474 kJ (1310 Cal)

Roast the fennel and sweet potato until they
have softened.

Cut a 15 cm (6 inch) round from each sheet of
shortcrust, using a saucer to help you.

Spoon the ricotta and Parmesan mixture into the
vegetable-filled pie tins.

sides

CHICKPEA AND ROAST VEGETABLE SALAD

Preparation time: 25 minutes +
  30 minutes standing
Total cooking time: 40 minutes
Serves 8

500 g (1 lb) butternut pumpkin, cubed
2 red capsicums, halved
4 slender eggplants, cut in half
  lengthways
4 zucchini, cut in half lengthways
4 onions, quartered
olive oil, for brushing

2 x 300 g (10 oz) cans chickpeas,
  rinsed and drained
2 tablespoons chopped fresh flat-leaf
  parsley

DRESSING
1/3 cup (80 ml/2 3/4 fl oz) olive oil
2 tablespoons lemon juice
1 clove garlic, crushed
1 tablespoon chopped fresh thyme

1 Preheat the oven to hot 220°C
(425°F/Gas 7). Brush two baking trays
with oil and lay out the vegetables in a
single layer. Brush lightly with oil.
2 Bake for 40 minutes, or until the

vegetables are tender and begin to
brown slightly on the edges. Cool.
Remove the skins from the capsicum if
you want. Chop the capsicum,
eggplant and zucchini into pieces,
then put the vegetables in a bowl with
the chickpeas and half the parsley.
3 Whisk together all the dressing
ingredients. Season, then toss with the
vegetables. Leave for 30 minutes, then
sprinkle with the rest of the parsley.

NUTRITION PER SERVE
Protein 8.5 g; Fat 12 g; Carbohydrate 20 g;
Dietary Fibre 7.5 g; Cholesterol 0 mg;
935 kJ (225 cal)

Rinse the chickpeas under cold running water
then drain thoroughly.

Chop the roasted capsicum, eggplant and
zucchini into small pieces.

Put the olive oil, lemon juice, garlic and thyme in a
bowl and whisk together.

CARAWAY POLENTA WITH BRAISED LEEKS

Preparation time: 10 minutes
Total cooking time: 30 minutes
Serves 4

6 cups (1.5 litres/48 fl oz) vegetable
   stock
1¹/₂ cups (225 g/7¹/₂ oz) polenta
2 teaspoons caraway seeds
45 g (1¹/₂ oz) butter
2 large leeks, cut into thin strips
250 g (8 oz) Fontina cheese, cubed

1 Place the stock in a large heavy-based pan and bring to the boil. Pour in the polenta in a fine stream, stirring continuously. Add the caraway seeds and then reduce the heat and simmer for about 20–25 minutes, or until the polenta is very soft.
2 Melt the butter in a frying pan over medium heat and add the leeks. Cover and cook gently, stirring often, until wilted. Add the Fontina, stir a couple of times and remove from the heat.
3 Pour the polenta onto plates in nest shapes and spoon the leeks and cheese into the centre.

NUTRITION PER SERVE
Protein 17 g; Fat 25 g; Carbohydrate 40 g;
Dietary Fibre 3 g; Cholesterol 72 mg;
1908 kJ (456 cal)

HINT: Ready-made stock can be quite salty, so use half stock, half water.

NOTE: Polenta is also known as cornmeal and is available from most supermarkets and delicatessens.

Use a sharp knife to cut the leeks into very thin, long strips.

Bring the stock to the boil, then pour in the polenta, stirring continuously.

Cook the leeks in the butter until wilted, then stir in the cheese.

GREEN BEANS WITH TOMATO AND OLIVE OIL

Preparation time: 10 minutes
Total cooking time: 25 minutes
Serves 4

⅓ cup (80 ml/2¾ oz) olive oil
1 large onion, chopped
3 cloves garlic, finely chopped
400 g (13 oz) can diced tomatoes
½ teaspoon sugar

750 g (1½ lb) green beans, trimmed
3 tablespoons chopped fresh flat-leaf parsley

1 Heat the olive oil in a large frying pan, add the onion and cook over medium heat for 4–5 minutes, or until softened. Add the garlic and cook for a further 30 seconds.
2 Add ½ cup (125 ml/4 fl oz) water, the tomato and sugar and season, to taste. Bring to the boil, then reduce the heat and simmer for 10 minutes, or until reduced slightly.
3 Add the beans and parsley and simmer for a further 10 minutes, or until the beans are tender and the tomato mixture is pulpy. Season with salt and black pepper, and serve immediately as a side dish.

NUTRITION PER SERVE
Protein 5.5 g; Fat 20 g; Carbohydrate 9.5 g;
Dietary Fibre 7.5 g; Cholesterol 0 mg;
992 kJ (237 Cal)

The garlic will be easier to chop if you smash it with the back of a knife first.

Cook the chopped onion in the olive oil until softened, but not brown.

Simmer the tomato mixture until reduced and slightly thickened.

LENTIL SALAD

Preparation time: 15 minutes +
  30 minutes standing
Total cooking time: 30 minutes
Serves 4–6

1/2 onion
2 cloves
11/2 cups (300 g/10 oz) puy lentils (see NOTE)
1 strip lemon rind
2 cloves garlic, peeled
1 fresh bay leaf
2 teaspoons ground cumin

2 tablespoons red wine vinegar
3 tablespoons olive oil
1 tablespoon lemon juice
2 tablespoons fresh mint leaves, finely chopped
3 spring onions, finely chopped

1 Stud the onion with the cloves and place in a saucepan with the lentils, rind, garlic, bay leaf, 1 teaspoon cumin and 31/2 cups (875 ml/28 fl oz) water. Bring to the boil and cook over medium heat for 25–30 minutes, or until the water has been absorbed. Discard the onion, rind and bay leaf. Reserve the garlic and finely chop.

2 Whisk together the vinegar, oil, juice, garlic and remaining cumin. Stir through the lentils with the mint and spring onion. Season well. Leave for 30 minutes to let the flavours absorb. Serve at room temperature.

NUTRITION PER SERVE (6)
Protein 13 g; Fat 11 g; Carbohydrate 20 g;
Dietary Fibre 7.5 g; Cholesterol 0 mg;
930 kJ (222 cal)

NOTE: Puy lentils are small, green lentils from France. They are available dried from gourmet food stores.

Stud the onion half with the cloves so that they are easy to remove after cooking.

Cook the lentils, then discard the onion, lemon rind and bay leaf.

Whisk together the vinegar, oil, lemon juice, garlic and cumin.

FRAGRANT GREENS

Preparation time: 15 minutes
Total cooking time: 8 minutes
Serves 4

2 tablespoons oil
300 g (10 oz) broccoli, cut into
    small florets
150 g (5 oz) snake beans, cut into
    short lengths
3 spring onions, sliced
250 g (8 oz) cabbage,
    finely shredded
1 green capsicum, cut into strips
2 tablespoons lime juice
1 tablespoon soft brown sugar
1/4 cup (15 g/1/2 oz) Thai basil,
    shredded (see NOTE)

1 Heat the wok until very hot, add the oil and swirl it around to coat the side. Stir-fry the broccoli and snake beans for 3–4 minutes, or until the vegetables are bright green and just tender. Add the spring onion, cabbage and capsicum, and continue stir-frying until just softened.
2 Combine the lime juice and brown sugar, stirring until the sugar has dissolved. Add to the wok with the basil. Toss to combine with the vegetables and serve immediately.

NUTRITION PER SERVE
Protein 6 g; Fat 10 g; Carbohydrate 9 g;
Dietary Fibre 7 g; Cholesterol 0 mg;
630 kJ (150 cal)

NOTE: You can include any suitable kind of green vegetable in this dish, including Asian greens. If you can't find Thai basil, use ordinary basil or coriander—either will give fragrance and flavour like Thai basil.

Top and tail the snake beans and cut them into short lengths.

Using a large sharp knife, finely shred the cabbage so that it will stir-fry quickly.

Shred the Thai basil just before you need it, or it will turn black.

SPICED SWEET POTATOES

Preparation time: 20 minutes
Total cooking time: 20 minutes
Serves 4–6

500 g (1 lb) orange sweet potatoes
3 tablespoons demerara sugar
3/4 teaspoon mixed spice
30 g (1 oz) butter, chopped
1/3 cup (80 ml/2³/4 fl oz) orange juice

1 Prepare a covered barbecue for indirect cooking at moderate heat (normal fire), see page 7. Peel the sweet potatoes and cut into thick slices. Arrange in layers in a shallow greased tray.
2 Sprinkle the sweet potato with the combined sugar and mixed spice and then dot with butter and sprinkle with the orange juice.
3 Cover the tray with foil, place on the top grill of the barbecue, cover and cook for 20 minutes, or until tender (remove the foil and test with a sharp knife; cook a few more minutes, if necessary). Sprinkle over a little more orange juice if drying out.

NUTRITION PER SERVE (6)
Protein 1 g; Fat 5 g; Carbohydrate 24 g;
Dietary Fibre 2 g; Cholesterol 13 mg;
566 kJ (135 cal)

Peel and thickly slice the sweet potato and arrange in a tray.

Sprinkle with the combined sugar and mixed spice, then dot with butter and orange juice.

Test the sweet potato with the point of a sharp knife and cook a little longer if not tender.

Purées & mashes

The success story of the humble mashed potato takes on a new twist with these delicious purées and mashes. These are simple to make and are perfect for soaking up the juices of home-made casseroles or as an accompaniment to lamb chops or juicy steaks.

CREAMED SPINACH PUREE

Wash and roughly chop 1 kg/2 lb) English spinach. Heat 60 g (2 oz) butter in a heavy-based pan and cook the spinach over high heat until it is wilted and the liquid has evaporated. Place in a food processor or blender with 1/2 cup (125 ml/4 fl oz) cream and purée until smooth. Season to taste with salt, pepper and nutmeg. Combine well and serve. Makes about 2 cups (500 g/1 lb). Serves 4.

NUTRITION PER SERVE
Protein 6 g; Fat 26 g; Carbohydrate 2 g; Dietary Fibre 8 g; Cholesterol 80 mg; 1114 kJ (266 Cal)

ROAST PUMPKIN PUREE

Preheat the oven to moderately hot 200°C (400°F/Gas 6). Seed 750 g (1 1/2 lb) pumpkin and cut into pieces. Place on an oven tray, brush with olive oil and roast for 35 minutes, or until the pumpkin is tender. Remove from the tray, cool slightly, then peel off the skin. Place in a food processor or mash with a masher until you have a purée, then add 1/4 cup (60 g/2 oz) sour cream. Season well. Makes about 2 cups (500 g/1 lb). Serves 4.

NUTRITION PER SERVE
Protein 4 g; Fat 9 g; Carbohydrate 13 g; Dietary Fibre 2 g; Cholesterol 20 mg; 623 kJ (149 Cal)

VERY COMFORTING CHEESY MASH

Cut 900 g (1 lb 13 oz) floury potatoes into chunks. Boil for 20 minutes, or until tender. Drain and transfer to a bowl. Add 2 crushed garlic cloves and 1/3 cup (80 ml/2 3/4 fl oz) cream, and mash, then beat until fluffy. Season. Stir in 300 g (10 oz) grated Gruyère or Cheddar and beat again until the cheese is melted. Makes 1 1/2 cups (500 g/1 lb). Serves 4.

NUTRITION PER SERVE
Protein 25 g; Fat 34 g; Carbohydrate 30 g; Dietary Fibre 4 g; Cholesterol 102 mg; 2220 kJ (530 Cal)

PEA PUREE

Melt 50 g (1¾ oz) butter in a pan over low heat and add 2 crushed garlic cloves. Stir briefly and then add 500 g (1 lb) frozen peas and cover. Increase the heat to moderate and, shaking the pan occasionally, cook the peas for 5 minutes, or until they are tender. Mash roughly with a masher or process in a food processor until you have a coarse purée. Season well. Makes about 2 cups (500 g/1 lb). Serves 4.

NUTRITION PER SERVE
Protein 7.5 g; Fat 11 g; Carbohydrate 8 g; Dietary Fibre 8 g; Cholesterol 32 mg; 650 kJ (155 Cal)

BEETROOT PUREE

Preheat the oven to moderate 180°C (350°F/Gas 4). Wrap 500 g (1 lb) unpeeled beetroot in foil and bake for 50 minutes, or until they feel soft to the touch. Cool, then peel off the skin and cut into pieces. Fry 1 chopped onion in 1 tablespoon olive oil until soft but not browned. Add the beetroot and 1 tablespoon balsamic vinegar and stir until heated through. Mash with a masher or in a food processor, then stir in 2 tablespoons cream. Makes 2 cups (500 g/1 lb). Serves 4.

NUTRITION PER SERVE
Protein 3 g; Fat 9 g; Carbohydrate 12 g; Dietary Fibre 4 g; Cholesterol 14 mg; 592 kJ (142 Cal)

BUTTERBEAN AND ROSEMARY PUREE

Heat 2 tablespoons olive oil in a frying pan over low heat and add 2 crushed garlic cloves. Stir briefly until softened, then add 4 x 300 g (10 oz) cans drained butter beans and 2 tablespoons chopped fresh rosemary and cook until heated through. Season well, then mash roughly with 2 tablespoons olive oil, until smooth. Drizzle with a little extra olive oil if desired. Makes about 1½ cups (375 g/12 oz). Serves 4.

NUTRITION PER SERVE
Protein 4 g; Fat 10 g; Carbohydrate 4 g; Dietary Fibre 6 g; Cholesterol 0 mg; 501 kJ (120 Cal)

Left to right: Creamed spinach purée; Roast pumpkin purée; Very comforting cheesy mash; Pea purée; Beetroot purée; Butterbean and rosemary purée.

KITCHEREE (SEASONED RICE AND LENTILS)

Preparation time: 15 minutes
Total cooking time: 25 minutes
Serves 6

1½ cups (300 g/10 oz) basmati rice
1½ cups (300 g/10 oz) split mung beans (mung lentils)
2 tablespoons oil
1 onion, sliced
3 bay leaves
1 teaspoon cumin seeds
2 pieces cassia bark
1 tablespoon cardamom seeds
6 cloves
¼ teaspoon black peppercorns

1 Wash the rice and lentils, then drain and set aside.
2 Heat the oil in a frying pan, add the onion, bay leaves and spices, and cook over low heat for 5 minutes, or until the onion is softened and the spices are fragrant. Add the rice and lentils, and cook, stirring, for 2 minutes. Pour in 1.25 litres water and salt to taste. Bring to the boil, then reduce the heat and cook, covered, over low heat for 15 minutes. Stir gently to avoid breaking the grains and cook, uncovered, over low heat for 3 minutes, or until all the moisture has evaporated. Serve hot with Indian curries.

NUTRITION PER SERVE
Protein 6 g; Fat 10 g; Carbohydrate 44 g;
Dietary Fibre 3 g; Cholesterol 0 mg;
1217 kJ (290 Cal)

NOTE: To avoid serving with the whole spices left intact, tie the spices in a piece of muslin and add it to the pan along with the boiling water. Discard when the dish is cooked.

Cook the onion and spices together until the onion is soft and the spices fragrant.

Stir gently until all the excess moisture has evaporated.

BARBECUED CORN IN THE HUSK

Preparation time: 15 minutes
Total cooking time: 40 minutes
Serves 8

8 fresh young corn cobs
1/2 cup (125 ml/4 fl oz) olive oil
6 cloves garlic, chopped
4 tablespoons chopped fresh parsley

1 Peel back the corn husks, leaving them intact. Pull off the white silks and discard. Wash the corn and pat dry with paper towels.
2 Combine the olive oil, garlic, parsley and some salt and black pepper and brush over each cob. Pull up the husks and tie together at the top with string. Steam over boiling water for 20 minutes, then pat dry.
3 Cook on a hot, lightly oiled barbecue grill or flatplate for 20 minutes, turning regularly. Spray with water during the cooking to keep the corn moist.

NUTRITION PER SERVE
Protein 3 g; Fat 15 g; Carbohydrate 15 g;
Dietary Fibre 3 g; Cholesterol 0 mg;
860 kJ (205 cal)

Carefully peel back the corn husks, then pull away the white silks (threads) and wash the corn.

Brush the oil, garlic, parsley and seasoning over the corn, then pull up the husk.

Tie the tops of the husks in place with kitchen string so they are secure.

147

HASH BROWNS

Preparation time: 30 minutes
Total cooking time: 15–20 minutes
Serves 4

800 g (1 lb 10 oz) waxy potatoes
(Desiree, Pontiac), peeled
120 g (4 oz) butter

1 Boil or steam the potatoes until just tender. Drain, cool, chop coarsely and season with salt and pepper.

2 Heat half the butter in a large heavy-based frying pan and put four lightly greased egg rings into the pan. Spoon the potato evenly into the egg rings, filling the rings to the top and pressing the potato down lightly to form flat cakes. Cook over medium-low heat for 5–7 minutes, or until a crust forms on the bottom. Be careful not to burn. Shake the pan gently to prevent sticking.

3 Turn the hash browns with a large spatula. Gently loosen the egg rings and remove with tongs. Cook for

another 4–5 minutes, or until browned and crisp. Remove from the pan and drain on paper towels. Add a little more butter to the pan, if necessary, and cook the remaining potato in the same way. Serve immediately.

NUTRITION PER SERVE
Protein 3 g; Fat 25 g; Carbohydrate 35 g;
Dietary Fibre 4 g; Cholesterol 75 mg;
1535 kJ (365 cal)

NOTE: If you don't have egg rings, cook as one large cake.

Fill the egg rings with the chopped potato and press the mixture down lightly.

Cook until a crust forms on the bottom. Be careful to prevent burning or sticking.

Use a large spatula to turn the hash brown over once a crust has formed on the bottom.

GRILLED HALOUMI AND ROAST VEGETABLE SALAD

Preparation time: 15 minutes
Total cooking time: 30 minutes
Serves 4

4 slender eggplants, cut in half and
　　then halved lengthways
1 red capsicum, halved, thickly sliced
4 small zucchini, cut in half and then
　　halved lengthways
1/3 cup (80 ml/2³/4 fl oz) olive oil
2 cloves garlic, crushed

200 g (6¹/2 oz) haloumi cheese, thinly
　　sliced
150 g (5 oz) baby English spinach
　　leaves, trimmed
1 tablespoon balsamic vinegar

1 Preheat the oven to hot 220°C
(425°F/Gas 7). Place the vegetables in
a large bowl, add 1/4 cup (60 ml/
2 fl oz) of the olive oil and the garlic,
season and toss well to combine. Place
the vegetables in an ovenproof dish in
a single layer. Roast for 20–30 minutes,
or until tender and browned around
the edges.
2 Meanwhile, cook the haloumi slices

on a hot, lightly oiled barbecue grill
for 1–2 minutes each side.
3 Top the spinach with the roast
vegetables and haloumi. Whisk
together the remaining oil and vinegar
to make a dressing.

NUTRITION PER SERVE
Protein 14 g; Fat 28 g; Carbohydrate 6 g;
Dietary Fibre 5 g; Cholesterol 26 mg;
1383 kJ (330 cal)

VARIATION: You can use any
roasted vegetable for this recipe. Try
orange sweet potatoes, leeks and
Roma tomatoes.

Roast the vegetables in a single layer until they
are tender and browned at the edges.

Cook the haloumi on a lightly oiled barbecue grill
for 1–2 minutes on each side.

Mix the remaining oil with the vinegar to make a
dressing for the salad.

CHARGRILLED ASPARAGUS

Preparation time: 5 minutes
Total cooking time: 3 minutes
Serves 4

500 g (1 lb) asparagus
2 cloves garlic, crushed
2 tablespoons balsamic vinegar
2 tablespoons olive oil
50 g (1³/₄ oz) Parmesan shavings

1 Break off the woody ends from the asparagus by gently bending the stems until the tough end snaps away. Cook the asparagus on a hot, lightly oiled grill or flatplate for 3 minutes, or until bright green and tender.

2 To make the dressing, whisk the garlic, vinegar and olive oil.

3 Pour the dressing over the warm asparagus and top with the Parmesan shavings and lots of black pepper.

NUTRITION PER SERVE
Protein 8 g; Fat 15 g; Carbohydrate 2 g;
Dietary Fibre 2 g; Cholesterol 10 mg;
700 kJ (165 cal)

To break the woody ends from the asparagus, hold both ends and bend gently.

Cook the asparagus on a hot barbecue grill until it is bright green and tender.

The easiest way to make Parmesan shavings is to run a potato peeler over the block of cheese.

ORANGE POPPY SEED ROASTED VEGETABLES

Preparation time: 20 minutes
Total cooking time: 50 minutes
Serves 6–8

500 g (1 lb) new potatoes, unpeeled, halved
6 parsnips, peeled and quartered lengthways
500 g (1 lb) orange sweet potato, cut into large pieces
335 g (11 oz) baby carrots, with stalks
6 pickling onions, halved

1/3 cup (80 ml/2³/4 fl oz) oil
2 tablespoons poppy seeds
200 g (6¹/2 oz) Brie cheese, thinly sliced

ORANGE DRESSING
1/2 cup (125 ml/4 fl oz) orange juice
2 cloves garlic, crushed
1 tablespoon Dijon mustard
1 teaspoon white wine vinegar
1 teaspoon sesame oil

1 Preheat the oven to moderately hot 200°C (400°F/Gas 6). Place all the vegetables and the oil in a large deep baking dish. Toss the vegetables to coat with the oil. Bake for 50 minutes, or until the vegetables are crisp and tender, tossing every 15 minutes. Sprinkle with the poppy seeds.
2 Whisk together all the dressing ingredients.
3 Pour the dressing over the warm vegetables and toss to coat. Transfer to a large bowl, top with the Brie and serve immediately, while still warm.

NUTRITION PER SERVE (8)
Protein 10 g; Fat 20 g; Carbohydrate 35 g; Dietary Fibre 6 g; Cholesterol 25 mg; 1510 kJ (360 Cal)

Quarter the parsnips lengthways and cut the sweet potato into large pieces.

Roast the vegetables until they are tender, then sprinkle with the poppy seeds.

Pour the dressing over the warm vegetables and toss to coat.

Glossary

Arborio rice is a special short-grain rice used for making risotto.

Balsamic vinegar is a rich, sweet and fragrant vinegar originating from Modena in Italy. Often used in dressings.

Bok choy (Chinese chard, Chinese white cabbage, pak choi) is a popular Asian green vegetable. The smaller type is called baby bok choy or Shanghai bok choy. Separate the leaves and wash well before use.

Broad beans (fava beans)

Butternut pumpkin (squash)

Cannellini beans (white beans, Italian white beans) are available canned or dried.

Capsicum (pepper)

Caster sugar (superfine sugar) is a fine white sugar with very small crystals.

Coconut cream and milk are extracted from the flesh of fresh coconuts. The cream is thick and almost spreadable. The milk is extracted after the cream has been pressed and is thinner.

Coriander (cilantro, Chinese parsley). All parts of this aromatic plant—seeds, leaves, stem and root—can be eaten.

Cornflour (cornstarch) is a fine white powder that is usually used as a thickening agent.

Eggplants (aubergines) come in a variety of shapes, sizes and colours. Slender eggplants are also called baby, finger or Japanese eggplants, while the most commonly used are larger and rounder.

English spinach (spinach) is sometimes confused with Swiss chard but is much more tender and delicate. Requires little to no cooking but should be washed several times to remove dirt.

Feta cheese is a soft, fresh goat's or ewe's milk cheese ripened in brine. It tastes sharp and salty.

Fish sauce is a brown, salty sauce with a characteristic 'fishy' smell. It is made from small fish that have been fermented in the sun. It is a popular seasoning in Southeast Asian cuisine. Use it sparingly as it has a strong flavour.

Flat-leaf parsley (Italian parsley, Continental parsley)

Green beans (French beans, string beans)

Hoisin sauce is a sweet, thick sauce made from fermented soy beans, flavoured with garlic and five-spice powder. Available in supermarkets.

Kaffir lime leaves (makrut lime leaves)

Kecap manis is a thick, sweet soy sauce. If unavailable, use regular soy sauce sweetened with a little soft brown sugar.

Lebanese cucumber (short cucumber)

Lemon grass is a thick-stemmed herb with pale leaves. It has a lemony flavour and aroma. Trim the base, remove the tough outer layers and finely chop the inner white stem.

Mirin is a sweetened rice wine and is available from Asian food stores. There is no real substitute.

Nori is dried seaweed that comes in sheets, either plain or roasted. Quick toasting over a naked flame freshens the nori and produces a nutty flavour.

Olive oil comes in different varieties suitable for different purposes. Extra virgin or virgin olive oil are most commonly used in dressings. Regular olive oils are preferred for cooking because of their neutral flavour. Light olive oil refers to the low content of extra virgin olive oil rather than lightness of calories.

Parmesan is a hard cow's milk cheese used widely in Italian cooking. Sold either grated or in blocks, freshly grated has a much better flavour.

Pecorino cheese is a hard sheep's milk cheese. You can substitute Parmesan.

Plain flour (all-purpose flour)

Polenta (cornmeal) is ground dried corn kernels. It is most often made into a porridge and flavoured by mixing in butter and Parmesan cheese.

Rice vinegar is a clear, pale yellow, mild and sweet-tasting vinegar made from fermented rice.

Risoni is a small rice-shaped pasta often used in soups.

Rocket (arugula, rugula, roquette) is a leaf with a peppery flavour. Often used in salads.

Roma tomatoes (egg tomatoes, plum tomatoes) are favoured for canning and drying because they have few seeds and a dry flesh. Ideal in sauces and purées. Sometimes called Italian tomatoes.

Self-raising flour (self-rising flour) is plain flour with baking powder added.

Shiitake mushrooms are Asian mushrooms with a dark brown top. Available fresh or dried from supermarkets or Asian food stores.

Snow peas (mangetout) are a variety of garden pea, eaten whole after being topped and tailed.

Spring onion (scallion, shallot). These immature onions have a mild, delicate flavour, and both the green tops and the white bulbs can be eaten raw or cooked.

Tamari is a naturally brewed, thick Japanese soy sauce; some varieties are wheat-free.

Tahini is a thick oily paste derived from ground sesame seeds. It adds a strong nutty flavour.

Thick cream (double cream, heavy cream) has a minimum fat content of 48% and some brands have gelatine added to them to give more body.

Tofu (bean curd) is an excellent source of protein. It comes in varying consistencies, each suitable for different cooking methods (follow the recipe). Fresh tofu doesn't have much taste but absorbs flavours from the food it is cooked with.

Tomato paste (tomato purée, double concentrate)

Wasabi paste has a pungent taste similar to horseradish.

Zucchini (courgette)

Index

Published by Murdoch Books®, a division of Murdoch Magazines Pty Ltd.

Murdoch Books® Australia
GPO Box 1203
Sydney NSW 2001
Phone: + 61 (0) 2 4352 7000
Fax: + 61 (0) 2 4352 7026

Murdoch Books UK Limited
Ferry House
51–57 Lacy Road
Putney, London SW15 1PR
Phone: + 44 (0) 20 8355 1480
Fax: + 44 (0) 20 8355 1499

Editorial Director: Diana Hill
Project Manager: Zoë Harpham
Creative Director: Marylouise Brammer
Designer: Michelle Cutler
Production: Fiona Byrne
Recipes developed by the Murdoch Books Test Kitchen.

Chief Executive: Juliet Rogers
Publisher: Kay Scarlett

The Publisher gratefully acknowledges the contribution of the recipe writers, chefs,
photographers and stylists who worked on the material appearing in this publication.

National Library of Australia Cataloguing-in-Publication Data
Everyday vegetarian. Includes index. ISBN 1 74045 212 7.
1. Vegetarian cookery. (Series: Everyday series (Sydney, NSW)).
641.5636.

PRINTED IN CHINA by Toppan Printing Co. (HK) Ltd.
Printed 2003.

IMPORTANT: Those who might be at risk from the effects of salmonella food poisoning
(the elderly, pregnant women, young children and those suffering from immune deficiency diseases)
should consult their GP with any concerns about eating raw eggs.